Supplemental Grammar Keys;
Dialogue Guide
and
Selected Workbook
Answers
for
Martin and Sokolova's
Russian Stage Two

Original material © 1995 by Nathan Longan

KENDALL/HUNT PUBLISHING COMPANY
4050 Westmark Drive   Dubuque, Iowa 52002

CREDITS

Design, Cover and Illustrations by:
Tatiana Zagorskaya

Photo Credits:
© Albert Lekhmus

Содержание

Introduction

This material is coordinated with Martin and Sokolova's Russian textbook <u>Stage Two</u>. It can be used by teachers and/or students. The first part of the material consists of translations of the base dialogues and short explanations of the functional tasks, lexical items and grammatical material that the dialogues practice. The second part provides answers to many of the written exercises.

Part One can help students master the material of the dialogues by providing them with a measure of confidence that they understand the meaning of the assigned oral exercises. Word for word, or "structural" translations often sound very akward, or simply unacceptable; these translations strive to be meaningful. Explanations are often provided where the translation and the structure of the original differ markedly. The explanations following the translations are aimed at elucidating the particular functional, content and accuracy points touched on in the exercises. Besides brief grammar points, many of the short explanations point out where recycled material has been introduced earlier, and where in the appendices more information can be found. Some of the explanations also include the correct forms needed to complete the oral substitution/transformation exercises. A few cultural notes are also included. Many of the "explanations" include exhortations to learn certain forms and memorize particular turns of phrase.

Teachers or students should emphasize or ignore the exhortations as their programs require. The exercises are numbered and bulleted as they are in the main text.

Part Two consists of answers to written exercises from the workbook. This section can be used either by teachers for quicker correction, or by students in programs that use self correction. Students can be asked, for instance, to compare their answers to the book and self correct in contrasting ink.

Nathan Longan

1.2▶

> ## Let's get acquainted.
> ## My name's John.

1.
Let's get acquainted.   My name is Sasha.   And you?
—My name is Linda
—Very nice (to meet you)
—I'm also happy to make (your) acquaintace.

The grammar here is straightforward. Mostly you have to learn the phrases. Notice that the "Let's get acquainted" uses the perfective future for the "acquainted" part. The "you" in "And you?" is in the accusative. Hopefully you remember that the construction "Как вас зовут" is an accusative one. The last two lines of the dialogue are two ways to register polite acknowledgement. Learn them.

2.
—Do you know what that person's name is?
—No, I don't know what their name is. I'm not acquainted with him.

This dialogue practices the use of the accusative when inquiring about a person's name. The last sentence provides a little practice with the instrumental: for now only the forms "с ней" and "с ним." The tough part is the accusative here: 1. эту девушку, 2. того молодого человека, 3. этого парня (there is a fleeting "e" here, and a soft stem), 4. ту девушку, 5. этого мальчика 6. эту дéвочку

The accusative case is somewhat difficult in that it is the one case where the "animacy" of the noun is important, but even animacy is only relevent in the plural and the masculine singular. For masculine inanimate nouns and adjectives describing them (and for inanimate plurals), the accusative forms coincide completely with the nominative forms.

The accusative case (animate and feminine):.

first(masc.& neuter) adj//noun: animate	second (mostly fem.) adj//noun	third (fem in -ь) noun	plural adj//noun: animate:
-ого//-его//-а/-я	-ую/-юю//-у/-ю	-∅ (no change)	-ых/их//various, see the appendices for details
first(masc.& neuter) adj//noun: inanimate is like nominative			plural adj//noun: inanimate is like nominative

3.
—Do you happen to know what that girl's name is?
—Yes, her name is Natasha.   You want me to introduce you to her?
—Sure [with pleasure]

Learn the construction "ты не знаешь" to express "Do you happen to know?". The second part of the second line gives us some more practice with the instrumental — here, the pronouns in the forms "с ней" and "с ним."

> **This is Natasha. She's my roommate. She's a student.**

5.
—Who is that nice young woman?
—That's Linda. She's a friend of mine.
—What's she do?
—She's a student.

The most important part of this mini dialogue is the line "What's she do?" It looks like "Who is she" but that doesn't make much sense in English. This exercise also provides practice with professions that will come in handy. Make sure you understand them all.

6.
—Where's he from?
—He's from America.
—So he's American?
—Yeah, he's an American.

This exercise practices countries in the genetive and names of nationalities. All the countries take из plus the genitive except Украина which becomes с Украины.

Since the early 1990s some politically sensitive Russians can in fact be heard to use the prepositions в and из with Украина, but most Russians still use the prepositions на and с.

For other nationalities see p. 376.

1.3▶

> **Linda doesn't speak Russian very well yet.**
> **Linda has been studying Russian for a year already.**

7.
—Do you know Spanish?
—I read (understand) Spanish, but I speak with difficulty.

This practices names of languages.

8.
—His native language is Spanish. He speaks Russian with a Spanish accent.

More languages and instrumental case practice.

9.
—As far as I know, he's German.
—Really? But he speaks Russian fluently, without an accent.

"As far as I know" is a handy phrase. Learn it. The rest of the dialogue provides practice in expressing how one speaks a language and saying "without an accent." (без takes a genitive complement.)

11.
—What do you do?
—I'm a student.
—Where do you go to school?
—I study at the University of Maryland.
—So what do you study?
—I study Russian.

Compare with dialogue 5 above. Both Russian sentences use Кто вы?; again, note that the Russian for "What do you do?" looks like what you might want to translate as "Who are you?" To render that same sort of rude sounding message in Russian, a Russian might change the word order and say, "А вы кто?" (using IC-4, of course), or they would ask more specifically Как вас зовут? Get used to saying Кто вы? when you want to ask somebody what they do. The other lines practice the use of verbs of studying and the prepositional and instrumental cases. Learn to say the majors listed.

1.4▶

```
┌─────────────────────────────────┐
│        No, that's not so.        │
└─────────────────────────────────┘
```

12.
—I thought you studied at Harvard in the humanities department, in your second year.
—Nope, that's not the way it is. I study at the University of Maryland in the philosophy department, and I'm in my third year already.

This exercises provides some longer sentences and stresses the phenomenon called "sequence of tenses." In English we say "-I thought you studi**ed**" whereas in Russian the present tense is used. If the sentense read Я думал, что ты учился... , the message would be, "I thought you had studied..."

Furthermore, we practice the use of the prepositional and the names of departments, and what year of study one is in, на каком курсе?

13.
—Do you study Russian?
—Yes, Russian is my major.

This is practice with the names of various majors. The word специальность is used to indicate one's "major." The traditional American undergraduate liberal arts curriculum is very broad and unfocused from the Russian perspective, but специальность and "major" are fairly close equivalents.

14.
—Do you happen to know what he does?
—You mean for a job? Yeah, he's a mathematician.

Compare dialogues 5 and 11, above. Again, the use of "Кто он?" for "what he does?" Here both the ambiguity of the literal sense "Who he is?" and the usual meaning of the words is made clear by the answer. Learn to pronounce the professions listed, and learn what they mean.

15.
—What's Lena's field?
—She's a psychologist
—Really? I didn't know.
—Yes, she's a specialist in child psychology.

Here we practice another way to talk about somebody's profession. Note the use of the construction у Лены when we use a possessive in English. The other important point here is the use of the dative case construction по. Don't get the words специалист and специальность confused. The first means "specialist" the later "specialty" or "field or area of expertise" "A specialist in ..." is expressed with the construction "специалист по (plus, of course, the dative of the speciality)."

Review the forms of the dative, if you don't know them, learn them, commit them to memory, NOW:

For first declension nouns (masculine or neuter) the endings are -у/ю.

For second declension nouns (the ones that end in -а in the nominative, often called "feminine" even though the group includes such masculine nouns as Володя, папа, and дедушка), the dative ending is -е.

For third declension nouns (feminine in мягкий знак) the dative singular ending is -и.

The dative plural ending for all nouns is -ам/ям.

The masculine adjective dative ending is -ому/ему.
The feminine adjectival ending is -ой/ей.
The plural dative adjectival ending is -ым/им

The dative case:

first(masc.& neuter) adj//noun	second (mostly fem.) adj//noun	third (fem in -ь) adj//noun	plural adj//noun
-ому/-ему//-у/-ю	-ой/-ей//-ой/-ей	-ой/-ей//-и	-ым/им//-ам/-ям

1.5▶

16.
—Do you know Oleg?
—Which Oleg?
—Well, Oleg. Oleg the mathematician.
—I didn't know that he was a mathematician.
—Yeah, Oleg's a top-notch specialist.

This dialogue gets us to practice using the accusative case for peoples' names, and a little practice using complex sentences. Not very complex, but the practice is good. It also gets us to use the conversational phrase "прекрасный специалист."

17.
This is an insurance agency. Bill works in the insurance agency.

Here we learn the names for various places of work and practice the use of the prepositional case. If you need to, review it.

The prepositional case:

most first (masc&neuter) adj//noun	most second (mostly fem.)adj//noun	third (fem in -ь) adj//noun	plural adj//noun
-ом/-ем// -е	-ой/-ей// -е	-ой/-ей// -и	ых/их///ах/ях
nouns that end in -ий and -ие in the nominative take -ии in the prep.	nouns that end in -ия in the nom. take -ии in the prep.		

19.

—**What do you do?**
—**I work for an insurance company.**
—**Are you the director?**
—**No, I'm just an insurance agent.**

Here again is the use of the phrase "**Кто вы**" for "What do you do?." Also note that while in English we can say either "I work for an insurance company," or "I work in an insurance company," in Russian the best way to get this message across is with the construction here. The rest of the dialogue is practice with names of posts in the given places of work. Learn both the places and the posts.

20.

—**My friend is a salesperson.**
—**Your friend works as a salesperson?**
—**Yes, he works in a store.**

Here we have some more professions and places. The grammar here to learn is the instrumental after "**работать**." To work as somebody is expresses with **работать** and the instrumental case. Review the endings if you need to:

The instrumental case:

most first(masc.) adj//noun	most second (mostly fem.)adj//noun	third (fem in -ь) adj//noun	plural adj//noun
-ым,-им//-ом,ем,ём	-ой,-ей//-ой,-ей,ёй	-ой,-ей// -ью	-ыми,-ими//-ами,-ями

1.6▶

22.

—**Do you live in a dorm?**
—**No, I rent a room not far from the university**

This exercises work on the conjugation of the verb **снимать**. The verb is imperfective and conjugates quite simply: **снима́ю, снима́ешь, снима́ет, снимаете, снимают**. The subject and verb are the only things that changes here, the rest is repitition of a phrase that uses the genitive. Just repeat it.

23.

—**Where do you live?**
—**I live not far from here.**
—**Do you rent a room?**
—**No, I live with my parents.**

Again, only the subject and verb change here. The phrase "**с родителями**" is repearted so that you get used to saying something in the instrumental plural.

24.

—**I heard you live in the dorm.**
—**Nope, that's not right. I rent a room.**

This exercise practices the conjugation of **снимать** and **жить (живу, живёшь, живёт, живёте, живут)**, you should have no trouble with this.

25.

This is Moscow University. Professor Ivanov works at Moscow University.

This exercise provides more practice with the prepositional case. You will need to decide what verb to use as well. By uderstanding what the places are you should be able to choose the most appropriate verb-**жить, работать, учиться**.

26.

Mama used to work in the drug store, but now she works in the post office.

This exercise provides still more practice with the places people can work and live. It also contrasts past and present forms. Note that the idea expressed by the English "used to..." is expressed with the adverd раньше, and the past tense. The past should not be too much trouble: жить goes to **жил, жила́, жи́ли,** учиться goes to **учи́лся, учи́лась, учи́лись**, and the past of **рабо́тать** is too simple to reproduce here. Some of the places take the preposition **в,** other take **на.** The following list will help, and you must learn these:

на бирже	in the stock market
на окраине	on the outskirts
на факультете	in the school(of biology)
на Аляске	in Alaska
на заводе	in the factory (plant)
на курсах	lessons
на Гава́йских острова́х	in Hawaii
на Кавказе	in the Caucasus
на улице	on a street
на Урале	in the Urals
в гора́х	in the mountains

27.

—I was told that you live in the center of Washington.
—No, that's not so. I live on the outskirts.

This practices a convenient way to express the passive voice ("I was told") and the rest of the dialogue practice the prepositions and some more places as well as the right way to introduce a contrary assertion "**Нет, это не так.**"

1.7▶

29.

—Do you have a sister?
—Yes, I have one sister and two brothers.

Here we practice the use of the cases with small numbers and common (though not easily predicatable) friends and relations. Remember that **один** changes to **одна** and **два** changes to **две** before feminine nouns. However, don't forget that **дедушка** and **дядя** are masculine so you won't use **одна** or **две** before them. **дедушка** and **дядя** are, though, second declension nouns so they will take the normal genitive singular form after **два: два дедушки, два дяди.** This holds for all masculine "second declension" nouns: Make sure you know the forms for the other nouns here.

30.

—Who is this in the center of the picture?
—That's my mother.
—How old is she?
—She's 43.

Here we practice the dative case of singular pronouns and the forms of the word **год: год, года, лет.** You should remember that **год** is used after 1,21,31 and so on. **года** is used after 2,3,4, 22,23,24,32,33,34 and so on. **Лет** is used in all other instances.

31.

—Does your friend have a computer?
—No, unfortunately, he doesn't have a computer.

More practice with the genitive here. The genitive of the possesive pronouns and nouns in the construction of the type "**у вашего друга**" and the genitive of singular nouns. Don't forget that **отец** has a fleeting [o]. For your information the endings for the genitive are:

most first(masc.&neuter) adj//noun	most second (mostly fem.)adj//noun	third (fem in -ь) adj//noun	plural adj//noun
-ого/-его//-а/я	-ой/-ей//-ы/и	-ой/-ей//-и	-ых/их//∅, ей, ов, ев, ёв

32.

—Do you have a sister?
—No, I have neither a brother nor a sister.

Here we have the genitive singular again, plus the construction **ни ...**, **ни ...**

33.

—I don't know anybody who is a mechanic. Do you happen to have a mechanic friend?
—Yes, I know one mechanic.
—Give me his phone please.

Oh, joy! The genitive plural! We have to learn at least these forms, and for homework even more. Since indicating negation is one of the main functions of the genitive, we have to use it here. Remember that if the noun ends in a vowel in the nominative singular (**книга, мама, общежитие, письмо**) it will have a zero (∅) ending in the genitive plural. A zero ending means that it will end in a consonant. Thus these four words will be **книг, мам, общежитий, писем**. The first two are pretty easy to see— you just drop the **-а**.

To see why **общежитие** becomes **общежитий** we must remember, or learn, that the final **-е** in **общежитие** is a disguised **о** (basic [o]). This **о** is added to the suffix **-ий** (which is added to the combined roots **общежит+** to make a noun). When we add **о** to **-ий** you would expect to get **иё** (**ий** + **о** = **иё**). However, **ё** is only **ё** when it is under stress (**моё, живёт**) so here the equation looks like this: **ий** + **о** = **ие**. Now if we drop only the basic sound "o" from the ending we end up with a zero ending: **общежитий**. **Письмо** becomes **писем** because of a fleeting basic [o], which, for the same reasons that decribe **общежитие**, becomes **е**. The same explanation holds for nouns that end in **-ия**, like **история** and **лаборатория**. In the genitive plural these nouns drop the basic [a] and leave the consonant **й** to produce **историй** and **лабораторий**.

If the linguistic approach hinders rather than helps, then learn that nouns ending in **-ие** or **-ия** take **-ий** in the genitive plural.

If the noun has a soft consonant ending or ends in a husher or sibilant (**ш,щ, ж, ч** — BUT NOT **Ц**!!!) in the nom. sing. (**преподаватель, словарь, врач, гараж**) it will take **-ей** in the genitive plural (**преподавателей, словарей, врачей, гаражей**). If the noun ends in a hard consonant in the nominative singular (**студент, учебник**) then it takes **-ов** in the genitive plural. Noun stems in **ц** (**американец**, and lots of other nationalities) take **-ев** — **американцев**. The ending **ёв** occurs in rare "irregular" forms (for the very curious, here are two: **дядьёв, зятьёв**), but in this exercise there are no real surprises.

Do note that **медсестра** is **медсестёр** in the genitive plural.

Whatever way you choose to learn the genitive plural, it is time to master it.

34.

—Do you have a textbook?
—Yes, I have a textbook.
—So where is it?
—It's on the table.

Here you are to complete the dialogues. This will require replacing the noun with the appropriate pronoun and then putting the place into the prepositional case.

1.8▶

36.

—You're funny!
—I'm funny!? No, it's you that's funny.

This is simply a dialogue to practice various descriptions of people: emotional, physical, intellectual. You must learn all these words.

37.

—That's funny!
—You think that's funny? It's not funny to me. I think it's sad.

Notice here the difference between the English/American expression of emotion using the construction "I think" and the Russian dative construction. Otherwise, this exercise is purely for practice of adverb pairs that are used in dative constructions to express emotional relationship to something. You must learn these all if you don't know them.

38.

—That was funny.
—Maybe it was funny to you, but for him it was sad.

Note that the English translation adds the word "Maybe." This is the natural way for us to express what is being said in Russian. Here we also add the dative of personal pronouns in these dative construction of personal states with the added complication of being in the past tense (in the neuter). The dative case of the personal pronouns is: **мне, тебе, ему, ей, нам, вам, им.** You must know these.

If you don't know the meaning of all these "states of being" learn them:

скучно	boring
весело	fun
трудно	hard
легко	easy
просто	simple
сложно	complicated
обидно	offensive, hurtful
всё равно	all the same
удобно	convenient, comfortable
неудобно	inconvenient
понятно	understood

39.

It was fun in class.

Here we're just describing "how it was" in different places. Note the use of the prepositional for places (note the use of **в аэропорту́**) and also note that "at a person's place" is expressed with the construction "**у Бори́са**" etc...

Урок 2   Устные упражнения

2.2▶

1.

What is located where?

This is an exercise in spatial relations. We need to learn for active command all these prepositional phrases and the cases they govern.

слева от	to the left of	genitive
за	behind	instrumental
справа от	to the right of	genitive
рядом с	next to	instrumental
напротив	opposite	genitive
между	between	instrumental
близко к	near to	dative
недалеко от	not far from	genitive

3.

—Where are those boys hurrying to?
—They're running to school.

Here we are comparing verbs of motion with the means of transportation. Each will use a diffent verb of motion because of the different mode of transport: by foot (hurrying, running) to classes, flying (for airplanes), плыть for any water going vessel. The only one that is a little confusing is поезд, but we can get used to the idea that it takes идти, as does автобус. All these sentences require the unidirectional VoM since we are talking about motion in one direction at one time and the intention of the speaker is to indicate this.

5.

—Are you often at your friends' place?
—Yes, I go to their place quite often.

Here we are practicing the use of the multidirectional VofM ходить and getting some practice using у plus genitve for "at a person's place" and к plus the dative for expressing "to a person's place."

6.

This exercise offers practice contrasting the usages of unidirectional and multidirectional VofM. The basic concept should be familiar to you, and perhaps the only one that really needs explaining is 5 where the tendency to use the multidirectional for repeated action forces us to use the multidirectional even when going in one direction. Please work through these and figure out what they mean.

2.3▶

7.

These are more practice contrasting multidirectional and unidirectional. Make sure you know what they say since you will need to complete the sentences so that they make sense. (пешком - on foot, штраф-fine)

8.

Again, more practice with the multidirectional and unidirectional with repeated action and a single action in the past where the emphasis is on the action, not the round trip.

9.
—When did you meet up with your friend?
—I met up with my friend when I was on my way to the stadium.

You are here expected to form a dialogue in which, using the options provided, ask a question about when something happened or was done (meet somebody, spoke about 'this' with her, lost money, see John, remember about the meeting, start to rain, gasoline run out). The response should be logical; don't say that the gas ran out when you were walking to stadium, but otherwise the sentences can be, should be, your own.

12.
We are driving to the city. We are driving about the city

Here the contrast between the unidirectional and multidirectional underscores the idea of direction implicit in the unidirectional whereas the multidirectional may be used to indicate random-like movement in a certain place. To express this "indeterminate" meaning of driving, walking, runnning, etc... "in a given place" use the mulitdirectional verb plus the preposition по plus the dative (naturally). The places here are: city, room, garden (сад), center of the city, forest, court yard, Moscow.

13.
Linda is waiting for Sasha by the circus.
She is walking around (by) the circus.

The car is headed for the city center.
The car is going to the city center.

Change the rest of the sentences similarly.

1. Boris saw his acquaintance and wants to talk with him. [Change it to something like, "Boris is going toward his friend."]
2. Natasha is descending the stairs. [N. is going down].
3. He is waiting for a call and can't sit in one place. [He is walking around the roon.]

These sentences require some work to come up with a meaningful sentence that conveys the basic meaning. You may find that you have to spend more time on this than on other sentences.

2.4▶

14.
Do you like to walk?

This whole exercise is devoted to situations where the general, basic act of walking, flying, swimming, running, etc... is mentioned. This use requires the multidirectional. Try and figure out the meaning of all these little dialogues and understand why each case requires the multidirectional.

17.
—Yes, I went to the doctor's.
—Were you at the doctor's?
—Yes, I went to the doctor's.

This exercise can be compared to ex. 5 where we had **бывает** in the present tense shown to be similar to (if not downright synonymous with)the multidirectional verb of motion in the present. We have a similar situation here, but in the past tense. Here the multidirectional in the past means one round trip. (in a different context the multidirectional might mean many round trips, but here it means only one, and we understand this from the context).

18.

Here you need to supply the right form of a "to go by foot" verb in the right tense. (The first dialogue is about going to a ceramics exhibit in the "House of Artists"; the second dialogue is about where somebody was when the first person called and couldn't get in touch—дозвониться—with the second. The third dialogue is about going to Washington and why—зачем)

19.
—Did you see your parents last week?
—Yes, I went (to visit) them.

This exercise, like 13, requires that you provide appropriate answers using a verb of motion. Again, it may take a little longer since you need to understand what is being asked. Make sure you understand what is being said and have prepared appropriate answers.

2.5▶

20.
—Are you going with those books to the library?
—Yes, I'm carrying these books to the library.

We are here introducing the transitive verbs of motion, нести, вести, везти (unidirectional) and носить, водить, возить (multidirectional). Here all the examples ask for a unidirectional. Learn how to conjugate these verbs. The sentences are pretty straightforward. You should know all the words.

21.

Here you need to fill in the appropriate transitive verb of motion using the cues provided in the dialogues.

22.
—Does he usually go to classes with a dictionary?
—Yes, he usually carries a dictionary to classes.

In these sentences the intransitive verbs of motion used in the questions need to be changed to transitive VoM and the objects from prepositional phrases to direct objects. Make sure you know which verbs go with which motion. Notice that since all these questions ask about usual behavior that the VoM are all multidirectional (both the transitive and intransitive). The multidirectional transitive VoM are возить (to transport by vehicle, this includes leading when the leader is on foot and the led is in, say, a wagon or when you are pushing a cart), водить (to lead on foot-both leader and led), носить (to carry). Learn their conjugations (yes, the first person singular of возить and водить are the same):

носи́ть	води́ть	вози́ть
ношу́	вожу́	вожу́
но́сишь	во́дишь	во́зишь
но́сит	во́дит	во́зит
но́сим	во́дим	во́зим
но́сите	во́дите	во́зите
но́сят	во́дят	во́зят

The words that you should know but might not in this exercise include: деньгами (from деньги-money), почтальон (from почта, "mailman" —mailmen deliver newspapers as well as letters in Russia—and they do it twice a day), детьми (from дети-children). If you are unfamiliar with the instrumental plural forms of дети and деньги, you should learn them here.

> **The passerby answered and walked, or, more precisely, ran on; he was probably in a hurry.**
> **Sasha invited me to go with him to the circus. This evening we are going [we will go] to the circus.**

The above examples reflect the use of the prefix по- to indicate what might be called a "factitive" meaning (as in "stating a fact") in the past, the infinitive and the future. With this meaning the prefix по- is added to the unidirectional verb and forms a perfective. (We will later encounter the use of this prefix temporally to mean "for a little while" when added to the multidirectional, but we'll leave that for a later date, lesson 10).

The по- here really has little semantic "load," (it doesn't add a particular direction or speed or much of anything else to the meaning of the verb) but is rather required by the grammar of constructions that need a perfective form. This use of the prefix **по-** is encountered in five main contexts: 1. In the past and future when we describe inception of motion, e.g. "He got in the car and went downtown," 2. In the past and future when change of speed or direction is mentioned, e.g. We went straight then went left, We saw the school and went slower. 3. In the past and future in a sequence of actions, e.g. We went to the movies, then we went to a restaurant, then we went home. We'll go to the movies, then we'll go to a restaurant, then we'll go home. 4. In the form **пойдём** (and its colloquial, less formal and more immediate **пошли**) when we mean "let's go" or "shall we go" "wanna go together". This is sometimes refered to as the first person imperative. 5. In the infinitive after **хотеть** and after verbs of suggestion, invitation and proposition: I want to go to the movies. I suggest we go to the lake. She invited her to go to the theater.

Notice that in the first sentence above, when we want to express the inception of motion in the past we need a perfective and we get that by adding по- to the needed unidirectional VoM.

In the second sentence above we have the use of the perfective infinitive after a verb of inviting. In the third sentence we have a future meaning.

In exercises 24-27 we practice all these five uses of the perfective verbs of motion with the prefix **по-**.

(We will later encounter the use of this prefix to mean "for a little while," but we'll leave that for a later date).

2.6▶
2 4 .
He got in the taxi and went to the train station.

Here we practice the use of the по- prefixed VoM in various situations in the past. In parentheses are reasons that the prefective in **по-** is needed. The most common situations are inception of motion and change of direction or speed.

The sentences are:

1. We decided to see the ballet "Swan Lake" and ... to the Bolshoi theater. (inception of motion)

2. The students passed the exams and .... home. (inception of motion)

3. Linda went into the metro, took a seet in the subway car and .... to downtown. (inception of action)

    4. They were going straight ahead and then ... left. (change of direction)

    5. The truck was going slowly and then ... faster. (change of speed)

    6.The kids saw mom and ... to meet her. (inception of motion)

    7. The car was going fast but in front of the school it .... slower.(change of speed)

    8. The tourists tooks seats in the bus and ... on the excurison.(inception of motion)

25.

There should be no unknown words here. If there are, you should learn the ones you don't know. In part "b" you should make sure you can get all the words in the right form. The prefix по- here is used in a sequence of actions.

26.

—On Sunday I want to go to the theater. Shall we go together?

—Unfortunately, I can't. On Sunday I'm going to the circus.

Here we have an infinitive in по- after **хотеть** and then a **пойдём** as a mild first person imperative or suggestion. In the response the speaker can't go, because they are going (in the future) somewhere else at that time.

The cues include three elements: a time and two places. The dialogue to be constructed should be built on the model above. None of cues have hard words. Words you don't know you should learn now or sooner if possible.

27.

—Did Sasha invite you to the movies?

—Yes, Sasha has invited me to go to the movies.

Here the prefix по- is used after verbs of invitation.The cues for this exercise are a person and an activity. The other main point is to compare the verbs предложить and пригласить. Note that they are very close in meaning in this context (предложить is often "translated" as "to propose"—obviously you can't really use that meaning in this context), but предложить takes a dative complement whereas пригласить takes an accusative.

2.7▶

28.

По- is, of course not the only prefix that can be added to VoM (though it is the only one that can have a purely factitive meaning). The other prefixes all add some special, mostly spatial, meaning to the verbs.

ONE KEY POIT: When prefixes are added to VoM the unidirectional/multidirectional distinction disappears: When a prefix is added to the unidirectional we get a perfective ; when added to a multidirectional we get an imperfective (Almost always—see chapter 10).

в- and вы- add the meaning, respectively, "to enter" and "to exit" usually an enclosed place and are often used with the prepositions в and из

за- adds the meaning of "dropping by" and is often used with the preposition в

об- indicates "circumnavigation" and is used without a preposition.

от- and под- indicate movement 'from and 'to' close proximity to the destination. Often the translations of verbs with these prefixes will be things that end in "up to" or "away from" as in "She came up to the man." "He walked away from the building." They must be used with the prepositions от and к (with these prefixes use these prepositions regardless of the nature of the destination - person, place or thing).

пере- adds the meaning of "going across or through" and is often used with the preposition через to indicated the barrier overcome.

13

при- and у- are used to describe movement often described as "arrival" and "departure."

про- and the preposition через (plus the accusative) adds meaning of "through" and про- and the preposition мимо (plus the genitive) adds the meaning of "by" or "past." (as in "He went by the house.")

This is also introduced in the WorkBook on page 17, ex. 5.

Read the paragraph and try to understand the meanings of the VofM therein.

> **I arrived at the meeting place on time.**
> **We were late for the show and left.**

29.

She will come over to my place today.   She often comes over
—Is Natasha going to be at your place tonight?
—Yes, she'll be coming over.
—Is she often at your place?
—Yes, she often comes over.

Note that to say someone is coming over "to someone's place" is a dative construction with к, The expression to be "at someone's place" is a genitive construction with у. We also contrast the future sense of the prefixed unidirectional in the nonpast with the imperfective of the prefixed multidirectional because of repeated action.

The prefix при- here is used for coming to somebody's place. It might also be for coming/arriving to a given place such as a train terminal, and verbs of motion with this prefix are often translated as "arrive".

30.

He usually leaves for work at this time.
—Where's Misha?
—He's not here. He's already left for work.
—Really?
—Yes, he usually leaves for work at this time.

The explanation here is similar to that for 29 except that the prefix is у-. Notice that there is no contradiction in the use of the prefix у- and going <u>to</u> someplace, such as "leaving for work."

This exercise also reviews the genitive of the personal pronouns.

> **I entered the room.**
> **I went out of the room.**

Note the cases and constructions above.

32.

No, he didn't come in, he just walked out.
—Has the teacher already gone into the classroom?
—No, he hasn't gone in, he just walked out.

You might imagine the situation here to be one in which the person asking the question is outside the lecture hall and doesn't see the professor in the hall so he asks if the professor has already gone in. The answer is that not only has he not just gone in, he has only just come out of the hall (for a smoke, say, before his next lecture).

The exercise is to contrast entering and exiting.

33.

No, he just drove out of the garage.
—Did the truck already drive into the garage?
—No, it just drove out.

The situation here must be imagined as similar to the one in 32.

—Ask Sasha to the phone please
—He's left. Call tomorrow.

—Ask Sasha to the phone please
—He's stepped out. Call back in about ten minutes

2.8▶

3 4 .

Where is she?
—Where is she?
—She's already left for work.
35. *Where is he?*
—Where is he?
—He's stepped out.
—Will he be gone long?
—No, he left to have a cup of coffee.

These two dialogues contrast the meanings of the prefixes **у-, вы-**. The first indicates a longer period of separation in both space and time. The second indicates a short "stepped out for a minute" meaning. None of cues should be problematic. Remember that for destinations that are people you need to use **к** plus the dative. Other destinations need **на** or **в** plus the accusative, except, of course, **дом** which as a destination is **домóй**. The cues for 35 are "to meet a friend," "to call home," "to fix coffee," "to fix tea," "to have a smoke," "to look at the event announcement." Note also the expression "идти в гости" (its an archaic accusative case, if you're curious about the classification of the form гости).

3 6 .

These should all be clear except perhaps the last part of 1.Подожди его....Wait for him.

Cars are coming up to the circus.
Cars are driving away from the circus
Spectators are running by me.

3 7 .

Are coming up to or going away from? Came up to or went away from?
Vocabulary

доска	chalk board
остановка	bus stop
остановиться	to stop
светофор	stop light
зеркало	mirror
вокзал	train station

The point here is to distinguish from the context what verb you will need—a present tense (hence imperfective) or a past perfective. You will have to understand the sentence before you can get the right word.

38.

a *Yes, the bus drives right up to this building.*
—Does the bus stop at this store?
—Yes, it drives right up to the store.

This exercise practices the use of the prefix под-. Since под- provides the meaning of "up to," i.e. proximity to but not actual arrival at, Russian uses the preposition к plus, of course, the dative after verbs of motion with the prefix под-.

b. *No, it drives by that building.*
—Does the bus stop at this store?
—No, it drives by this store.

39.

He went right by.
—Did he come up to you?
—No, he went right by me.

Here we use the prefix про- and the preposition мимо to indicate motion "past" something. In 39 we have the prefix-preposition pair под- / к to indicate "up to".

3.2▶

> **Linda got up this morning <u>at</u> <u>eight</u> o'clock**
>   **Linda usually goes to bed <u>around</u> <u>11</u> <u>pm.</u>**
>   **Linda's free <u>after</u> <u>6pm.</u>**
> **They study <u>from</u> <u>9</u> <u>to</u> <u>6</u>..**

1.

These are times that certain things happen. Remember these constructions: on the hour will be **в** plus the hour (**в два часа, в пять часов**). On the half hour will be **в половине** plus the genitive of the ordinal number of the following hour ("following" as we see it). So, "at 2:30" would be "at half of the third" or "**в половине третьего**".

For things that happen at times between the top of the hour and half past, use **в** plus number of minutes plus the genitive of the ordinal number of the following hour. "At 4:10" would sound like "At 10 minutes of the fifth"—**в десять минут пятого**.

For things that happen at times between the half hour and the top of the hour use **без** plus the genitive of the number of minutes followed by the cardinal of the approaching hour. That's a mouthful of an explanation, but what it means is that , "At 25 to 6" would be "Without 25 six" or "**Без двадцати пяти шесть.**"

2.
—**When did he go to bed?**
—**He went to bed late, at one.**

—**When did she get up?**
—**She got up early, at five o'clock.**

This exercise practices some common verbs needed to describe daily routine. They are very common and also, unfortunately, quite irregular or unusual. **лечь, встать, разбудить, проснуться.** (to lie down, to get up, to wake up somebody[i.e. transitive], to wake up yourself[i.e. intransitive]). They are all perfective. You'll need to know the imperfective forms (the imperfective infinitives are: ложиться, вставать, будить, просыпаться) as well, but right here we're working on the past of the perfectives. The perfectives conjugate as follows:

лечь	встать	разбудить	проснуться
ля́гу	вста́ну	разбужу́	просн́усь
ля́жешь	вста́нешь	разбу́дишь	проснёшься
ля́жет	вста́нет	разбу́дит	проснётся
ля́жем	вста́нем	разбу́дим	проснёмся
ля́жете	вста́нете	разбу́дите	проснётесь
ля́гу	вста́нут	разбу́дят	проснутся
лёг	встал	разбуди́л	просн́улся
легла́	вста́ла	разбуди́ла	просн́улась
легли́	вста́ли	разбуди́ли	просн́улись

3.
—Let's meet around eleven.
—Around eleven? Let's meet at eleven sharp.

This is a handy dialogue to learn for making appointments. Learn the construction "**Давайте встретимся**". The first part of the second line gives an example of a construction that is used to indicate approximation. Instead of using a word like "about" you can reverse the normal order and get the same, or an even better, effect. Learn the construction "**ровно в ...**" The next point to note here is that all the numbers need to be changed into the genitive. **семи, двух, трёх, десяти, шести, четырёх, пяти, восьми.**

4.
How about a little later, after five o'clock.
—Can you come at five o'clock?
—How about a little later. I'll be free only after five o'clock.

Here the phrase to learn is **Давай немного позже**. Notice that the translation is not "word for word," but you shouldn't be upset by such things by now. The time constructions here provide practice with "at a given hour" and "after a given hour." Make sure you can put these times into the genitive case.

5.
—Do you have classes every day?
—Yes, from nine o'clock.
　　Is this store open every day?
　　Is the pool open on Saturday?
　　Is the computer center open on Sundays?
　　Is the cafeteria open every day?
　　Is the legal affairs office open on Tuesdays?

This exercise gives you practice using the construction for "from a given hour." The construction is **С** plus the genitive case of the cardinal number. **С девяти, с пяти, с двух**. Notice that while in English we say a place is "open" the Russian uses a verb that we usually recognize as "to work"—**работать**.

6.
—Do you have classes every day?
—Yes, until three.
　　4. Is Prof. Leontief going to be in the department today?

This is the same as ex. 5, just that the construction is "to a given hour." The case is the same (genitive), but the preposition is **до**. **до девяти, до пяти, до двух**

3.3▶
7.
—When will the mechanic be here?
—From nine to one.

Now we combine these two constructions and come up with the phrase "from one given time to another."

8.

This paragraph gives an example of what you will need to be able to say about your day, what you did when (in "a") and what you do every day (in "b").

> **Linda goes to the pool on Monday and Wed.**
> **Linda came to Moscow in the fall, in Sept.**
> **The intensive course began last week.**

10.

—**When is your meeting?**
—**On Monday. We always have our meetings on Mondays.**
   1. sports practice, 4. day off

This exercise contrasts the use of the constructions "**в**" plus the accusative of the day for "on a day of the week" and **по** plus the dative plural for "on days of the week."

3.4▸

11.

—**Are they going to be in New York this week?**
—**No, they were already in New York, last week.**
   1. Is he taking the exam on the history of the Middle East <u>this</u> <u>semester?</u>
   3. Are you going to have a vacation this months?
   4. Is John going to work as a waiter this summer?
   5. Are Mary and Tom going to be in Moscow this Spring?
   6. Are you going to vacation (relax) at the sea this year?
   7. Are you going to meet with the correspondent from the paper "Moscow news" this week?

The words <u>week</u>, <u>semester</u>, <u>month</u>, <u>year</u> when used in the expressions "this (last, next, etc...) <u>week</u>, <u>semester</u>, <u>month</u>, <u>year</u>" to answer the question "when" are all prepositional case constructions. You need to know them and get used to using them. Practice these sentences. Note: **на неделе**, but all the others are **в** plus the prepositional.

12.

—**Do you have free time this week?**
—**This week, no. I'll have free time only next week.**

13.

—**Is Ira coming with us to the movies tomorrow?**
—**Unfortunately, no. She doesn't have any free time at all.**
   1. Is Misha coming over to your place tomorrow evening?
   2. Are you going to go with us on Tuesday to the rock concert?
   3. Are they going on an outing on Sunday? (зá город **means literally "out of the city," but it means into the countryside surrounding the big cities for outings)**
   4. Is Nadya going to be at Steve's party the day after tomorrow?
   5. Will you be able to go to this exhibit?

This exercise provides practice with phrases that will come in handy when you need to turn down somebody or explain why something can't be done (no time). Learn the phrases "к сожалению" and "совсем нет свободного времени."

14.
—Did you finish that article today?
—I didn't have any time to read today.
   2. to find
   3. to translate
   4. to type up
   5. to have a look at
   6. to put together (here, to write "a program")

This exercise provides a verb in the perfective, a time and an object. The dialogue consists of puting the cues together and adding the dative phrase **мне некогда было** plus the imperfective of the verb. This expression is another way of saying "no time." It is very common and useful, learn it, use it, love it. Note that in #2 the completion of "искать" (to search) will be "найти" (to find).

15.
—Has Linda lived in Moscow long?
—Yes, Linda has lived in Moscow since Semptember.

Here the cues are a person, an activity and a period "from which time" the activity has been performed. So, the first one would sound like this in English: "Has Misha studied English long?" "Yes, he's studied English since [he was in] school." The preposition **c** when it means from a certain time takes the genitive. All the time words should be in the genitive singular. If you need to review the genitive singular, the noun endings are: masculine/neuter:-**а,-я**. feminine: -**ы,-и**.

Linda came to Moscow for 10 months.
In ten months she'll go home.

Exercises 17-19 introduce and practice two more time expressions, both are accusative expressions— **на** plus the accusative of a time unit meaning "for a given amount of time" and **через** plus the accusative of a time unit meaning "in [or after] a given amount of time". The first one is the more difficult because in English the prepositionless phrase "I waited two hours" means the same thing as the phrase with a preposition "I waited **for** two hours." In Russian that thought can be expressed only **without** a preposition "**Я ждал два часа.**" The use of the preposition **на** plus the accusative is confined to expressions where an action is completed <u>before</u> the time begins. We might illustrate the situation like this:

an "ACTION" after which occurs	A TIME FRAME .	
ПРИЕХАЛ	**на три дня.**	arrived <u>for</u> three days
ЕДЕТ	**на две минуты.**	going <u>for</u> two minutes
ПРИЕДЕТ	**на неделю.**	coming <u>for</u> a week
ПРИГЛАСИЛ	**на месяц.**	invited <u>for</u> a month
ПРИГЛАШАЕТ	**на выходные.**	invites <u>for</u> the weekend
ПРИГЛАСИТ	**на́ зиму.**	will invite <u>for</u> the winter

Через plus the accusative is used when the action begins <u>after</u> the time frame. We might illustrate the situation like this:

A TIME PERIOD <u>after</u> which occurs	an ACTION	
Через месяц	**всё будет готово.**	<u>In</u> a month all will be ready
Через неделю	**я поеду в Москву.**	<u>In</u> a week I will leave for Moscow

Obviously, you don't want to be drawn into the trap of thinking that the phrase order has to follow the above illustrations; they just reflect the relation of the time and the action, not the order of the phrases.

3.5▶

1 7 .

—Did you come for a month
—No, I came for two months.

    4. Were you invited for a semester?
    5. Is Sasha leaving for two months?
    6. Have you come here [to us] for a long stay?
    7. Are your parents going to be gone long?

1 8 .

—When are you going to Washington?
—I'm going to Washington in March.
—And when are you coming home?
—In May.
—You're going for two months?
—Yes, I'm going to Washington for two months.

The only "new" point to note here is that "in a given month" is expressed with "в" plus the prepositional.

1 9 .

—When are you leaving?
—I'm leaving on the tenth of September.
—In ten days?
—Yes, I'm leaving in ten days.

The cues here are: the date of departure (given in the Russian style, date.month [in Roman numerals]) and then in parentheses the date the dialogue is spoken:
1. 16.VII [16th of July] (today is the second of July)—you should be able to figure out that there are fourteen days, or two weeks, to go.

2 0 .

—Are you going to be at the show?
—I'll get there fifteen minutes before the beginning of the show.

    2. the openning of the exhibit.
    4. reception at the embassy.

This exercise introduces the structure for expressing when something happens a certain amount of time before another event. The "something happens" in this exercise is "I will get there [arrive]". The structure is the prepositon **за** plus the accusative of the time expression followed by **до** plus the genitive. We mustn't be disturbed by the fact that the Russian expression uses two prepositions for this expression and the equivilant English only has one—that's just the way it is.

Linda works on her homework half an hour. Linda did her homework in half an hour.

Exercises 21-23 deal with the use of perfective and imperfective aspect in time expressions. You should recognize that the first sentence above describes a process with no indication one way or the other that the action was finished. In contrast, the second sentence clearly stresses that the action was completed. Ex. 21. provides a perfective sentence and you are to provide an imperfective using the time expressions correctly. Note that with the imperfective here we have no preposition, simply the accusative of the time unit.

21.
—She solved this problem in an hour.
—I was working on it for the whole evening.
1. She translated this complex text in a day.
2. She typed up the article in five hours.
3. Pasha memorized these verses in half an hour.
4. Anton prepared these experimental models in a month.
5. She wrote the computer program in a month.
6. My friend the physicist conducted the experiment in a week.
8. Olga compiled the schedule in five days.

22.
—Svetlana washed up for half an hour.
—And I washed up in ten minutes.
1. My sister was dressing for an hour.
2. They were getting into town for two hours.
3. Volodia was cleaning up his room all day.
4. Galya was preparing dinner for an hour and a half.
5. Marina was getting her things together for two days.
6. John typed his term paper for two weeks.

23
a. I didn't leave the house for three days because I was writing a computer program.

These exercises provide contexts and you are to choose either the imperfective or perfective conclusion depending on the context. Thus, in the example when we read "I didn't leave the house for three days because..." we know we should use an imperfective explanation because this is a "background" during which another action takes place. Look through the examples and make sure you understand the contexts.

We'll have time to have a cup of coffee.

Certain verbs, by virtue of their meaning, imply contexts that require the use of one aspect or the other. For instance успеть, "to have time to," "to manage," implies the completion of an action and will be followed by a perfective infinitive. On the other hand, verbs like начать, "to begin" and кончить, "to finish" should be followed by an imperfective infinitive. (I realize that this might sound a bit strange since we want to associate perfective aspect with stress on the beginning or end of something and these verbs начать, "to begin" and кончить, "to finish" seem to do nothing if not stress the beginning and end of an action. However, it must be realized that these two verbs are themselves perfective and the actions being begun or ended are logically in process, and thus logically imperfective.) Exercises 24 and 25 practice this point.

24.
—Did Mark finish his term paper?
—Yes, he managed to type it up yesterday
All of these sentences are found in previous exercises. The perfectives are:
перевести, просмотреть, собрать, составить, нарисовать, написать

25.
—Did you manage to memorize the words yesterday?
—No, I forgot to memorize them; I only started studying them today.
   You shouldn't have trouble providing the imperfectives of these verbs.

> When I was doing that, I remembered my dream.
> Last night, before going to bed, I set my alarm clock for seven o'clock.

   There are three complex time expressions to learn here. In English the expressions "**When** someone was doing something, they did something else" "**Before** someone did something, they did something else," "**[Right] before** someone did something, they did something else," and "**After** someone did something, they did something else" are all pretty simple; just put the adverb before the phrases. In Russian the equivalents are not quite so simple. Since Russian prepositions need objects the constructions are more complex. Instead of the one word "before" use the phrase **до того, как**. Instead of the simple "right before" use **перед тем, как**. Instead of the word "after" use **после того, как**

3.7▶

   27
a.
—When are you going for a walk?
—I'm going for a walk after I finish my homework.
б.
—When did you finish your homework?
—I finished my homework before I went out for a walk.
в.
Before answering, you must think.

> I dress, [and] wash my little sister, and comb [her hair].
> I quickly dress, wash and comb my hair.

   28.
   These sentences practice the difference between transitive verbs of hygene and grooming and their intransitive variants. Learn these verbs.

> After dinner I am always free.
> We were busy until two o'clock.
> He will be ready in five minutes.

   Exercises 29-32 practice the short form adjectives **свободен, занят, готов**. All three of these are very useful and need to be learned. They each come in masculine, feminine, [neuter] and plural forms. You need to know all the forms, but they are not hard. Just bear in mind that **свободен** has a fleeting **e**. Also note the stress on the feminine forms.
   The exercises also practice handy things like genitive with the prepositions **до** and **после**.
   29.
—When are you free?
—I'm free after dinner.
   30.
—Is Inna free after three?
—Unfortunately, no. She's busy after three. She's free until three.
   31.
—Linda, are you already ready?
—Just a minute. I'm not ready yet. I'm looking for my notebook.
   32.
—Can we have dinner?
—Yes, dinner will be ready in five minutes.

4.2▸

> Linda in general looks like her mother, but she has dark eyes like [her] father.
> Along side stood a pleasant young lady with long red hair.

1.

Who looks like whom?
—**Who does Sasha look like?**
—**He looks like his father.**

This exercise practices the use of the phrase most commonly used to describe "who someone looks like." The construction uses the short form adjective **похож** followed by the preposition **на** and the accusative case of the person or thing that is being introduced for comparison. The root of **похож** is **ход+** as in **ходить**, and you might remember the construction if you remember that the English "[your tie] *goes with* your shirt" also uses a verb of motion. You also might think of a phrase like "His looks *approach* those of his father." If neither of these help, just memorize the constructions.

2.

Not similar in looks to anyone, Doesn't look like anyone.
—**Does Volodya look like his mother or his father?**
—**He doesn't look like anyone, neither his mother or his father.**

This exercise simply practices the phrases. Don't worry too much about the "double negative," we'll return to it explicitly later.

3.

She has blue eyes, like her mother.
—**She has blue eyes, like her mother.**
—**Yes, she looks alot like her mother.**

This exercise provides descriptions of body parts and then has you compare a person to a relative with a similar body part and then generalize to the whole person. The body parts are: blue eyes, a straight nose, a large mouth, black hair, a pretty smile, green eyes, wide shoulders, straight white teeth. You should learn all these parts and the descriptions. Note that unlike the English construction, the Russian construction requires a preposition in the second part as well as the first — **У неё голубые глаза, как у мамы.** Note also that the words for straight with teeth and nose are different.

4.

—**Mama has green eyes and pretty lips.**
—**Vera looks like mother. She has the same kind of green eyes and pretty teeth.**

Here we practice more comparisons. We use the phrase **такие же** "same kind of." Notice that it is an adjectival phrase, and so you will need to make sure that you make it agree with the thing/things being compared.

5.

Who was standing by the window, the bench...?
A man with a round face, dark hair and a black mustaches [mustachios] was standing by the window.

Here we see, perhaps for the first time, the locational use of the preposition **y**. It means "next to" or "by." The other thing practiced here is the instrumental for description. Recall the endings for the instrumental:

	NOUNS	ADJ.
first declension (all masc. or neuter)	basic [-om] written either **-ом, -ём,** or **-ем**	basic [-im] written **-ым** or **-им**
second declension (mostly fem.)	basic [-oj] written either **-ой, ей,** or **ёй**	FOR FEMININE NOUNS: basic [-oj] written either **-ой, ей,** or **ёй** - yes, the same as for 2nd declension nouns
fem. III	basic [-'ju] written **-ью**	
plural	basic [-ami] written **-ами** or **ями**	basic [-imi] written **-ыми** or **-ими**

The places where the people are standing are: a bench, a table, a window, a board (black board), the entrance to an institute, a car.

6.

Who came into the lecture hall, the class...?
A tall person around twenty five came into the lecture hall.

Here we practice some of the things introduced in earlier chapters: a verb of motion followed by the accusative, the inversion of numbers and the things quantified for approximation (in this case years, but see exercise 3 chapter 3, p. 87, for examples with time). Note that this is a genitive construction (a person "of" so many years) so use **лет** in all these examples. (Remember that the question of using genitive singular after 2, 3, and 4 and their compounds applies only when the numbers are in the accusative or nominative). The genitive for the numbers will be: **десяти, двацати, шестидесяти, тридцати, сорока трёх, одиннадацати.** Learn these forms! [for the very curious I can let you know that if we were not inverting the word order and we had a form with **один**, the phrase would read, e.g.: **Человек двацати одного года**. With compounds of **один** Russians just won't use this inverted word order for approximation. If we approximate the phrase becomes **Человек около двадцати одного года.**]

The other element here is height. Russians often use a genitive construction that translates reasonably well into English as "of medium height" to describe a person's height. You should use it, too.

As with most of the exercises in this chapter we are using slightly longer sentences and introducing some slightly more complex description devices. The ability to describe in detail is a key skill that must be practiced extensively (for those interested, detailed description is a function characteristic of the Advanced level [ILR level 2]).

7.

Read this passage through and prepare to discuss the picture using the turns of phrase above.

8.

Prepare for class.

9.

Read and laugh.

4.4▶

10.

Which one? What's she wearing?
—Do you know who that woman is?
—Which one?
—In the blue suit.
—No, I don't.

Work on the prepositional case is the central grammar point of this exercise. Refer back to chapter one if you need to refresh your memory on the forms of the prepositional. Clothes and colors are the operative content point here. Learn all these pieces of clothing, and the colors:

black	glasses
light blue	jeans
purple	dress
yellow	overcoat
white	robes
grey	sports jacket
pink	blouse
green	shorts
brown	raincoat

11.

What kind of pants did he buy?
—Did Ed buy plaid (or checkered) pants?
—No, striped.

Here we practice three patterns — plaid, striped and polka dotted. All three patterns are expressed using an accusative construction в полоску, в клётку, в горошек. Learn them and use them often.

12.

What a pretty dress. You look very good in it. [It really becomes you].
—What a pretty dress!
—You like it?
—Yes, it really becomes you.
—Thanks for the compliment.

The phrase Оно тебе идёт is difficult to translate succinctly into contemporary American English, but it is a very useful and common phrase in Russian. It is a dative construction in Russian and sort of fits the "it becomes him" phrase in English, at least structurally.

   Make sure you know the articles of clothing. You should also be aware that saying "Thank you" in response to a compliment is not really the norm in Russian. Most Russians will downplay a compliment with some self depricating remark. It is not unheard of, however, and for this exercise we will stick to "Thanks for the compliment." The clothing articles are: tie, blouse, hat, shirt, sweater (not a cardigan), glasses, suit, overcoat, skirt,raincoat, windbreaker type jacket.

13.

—Buy that skirt.
—Which one? The grey plaid one? No, I don't like it.
—But it really becomes you.

Learn to use **тот, то, та, те** in the accusative. This is another indicative pronoun that refers to something slightly farther away than the something that would be refered to with the word **этот**. Otherwise, we're just practicing stuff we did above, now combining colors and patterns.

14.
Yes, she wears long dresses.
—**Does she wear long dresses?**
—**Yes, she wears long dresses.**

This dialogue points out two ways that the Russians use to describe habitual dress. The first construction uses the verb that we know so far as "carry"—**носить**. The second construction uses the verb **ходить** plus **в** plus the prepositional case for the thing worn (you might think of it as "goes around in jeans). Learn the articles of clothing.: tennis shoes, short skirts, pants, jeans, glasses.

15.
Why don't you wear the red dress?
—**Why don't you wear the red dress?**
—**I don't wear the red dress because it doesn't become me.**

Here we combine the phrases for wearing something with the "becomes her" construction.

> **I like the purple dress**
> **I liked it immediately. [I liked it as soon as I saw it.]**

4.5▶

16.
I liked it immediately. [I liked it as soon as I saw it.]
—**I like this purple dress. How about you?**
—**I liked it too right away.**

Nothing special to learn grammatically speaking here. Just learn the colors and articles of clothing and don't forget to make the verb agree with the subject. Notice that the reply uses the prefective **понравилось** which with the adverb **сразу** produces a meaning very close the English "It caught my eye right away."

17.
Who do you like?
Who likes you ?.
—**Do you like Sasha?**
—**Yes, I like him. [I find him attractive]**
—**And does he like you [Does he find you attractive?]**
—**I don't know if he likes me.**

Two points to ponder here. In the first place you need to conjugate the verb **нравиться** in the first and second persons which you haven't done before. In the second place you should begin to deal with the **ли** constructions. We've seen it before and we will see it again; get used to using it. (Review lesson 2, ex. 45 in the workbook if you need to).

It is the esteemed opinion of a number of observers of modern spoken Russian that the construction **нравлюсь ли я ему** is not a natural response for colloquial speech. Russians tend to omitt this rendition of direct speech altogether or start with it, in contrast to English, where it comes at the end. This is due to the basic governing principle of word order in Russian by which old information comes first and new information comes at the and of an utterance.

Ей нравится зелёный цвет? - Не знаю. or Нравится ли ей зелёный цвет? - Не знаю.

Им нравится русский язык? - Не знаю. or Нравится ли им русский Язык? - Не знаю.

18.
Prepare for class.

19.
Read and laugh

4.6▶

20.
On the contrary, she decided not to do that.
—Did she decide to go up [to him]?
—Did she decide to go up to him?
—On the contrary, she decided not to approach him.

This is an exercise in using the perfective and imperfective in the infinitive. Notice that the infinitive in each answer will be in the imperfective because the message is "advised, decided, promised, asked" NOT <u>to do</u> something.

You might notice that the words "advised, decided, promised, asked," unlike the infinitives, are not all of one aspect. This is an excellent example of how aspect is tightly interwoven not only with context but also with the semantics of the underlying action expressed in the verb. Thus, Она <u>решила</u> (совершенный вид) подойти (или, не походить). or Он <u>обещал</u> (несовершенный вид) подойти (или, не походить). In the first sentence the perfective is used because the idea of "deciding" is a "perfective" idea—its imperfective "решать" corresponds to "work on" "think about" and though in English might still be rendered as "decide" the context in English will make clear that the use is "imperfective." In the second example "to promise" is imperfective because the completion of that promise is not indicated here. The first example here would sound like this in English: "Did he promise to tell about that?" "On the contrary, he promised not to tell about that." Whether or not the promise was kept is not indicated.

The various verbs are: promised, decided, asked, advised. The various action to be done or not to be done are: tell about that, drop by Natasha's, talk about this with Sasha, leave early, buy him that suit, clean up the room, gather his things, put on the purple suit. Learn the pairs. If you don't know their meanings, learn them. The pairs for exercises 20, 21, 22, 23 are:

imperfective	perfective
рассказывать	рассказать
заходить	зайти
говорить	поговорить
уезжать	уехать
покупать	купить
убирать	убрать
собирать	собрать
надевать	надеть
брать	взять
делать	сделать
узнавать	узнать
спрашивать	спросить
писать	написать
переводить	перевести
отрывать	открыть
включать	включить

21.

No, I decided not to do that.
—**Did you buy those shoes?**
—**No, I decided not to buy those shoes.**

Again, this exercises works on the use of aspect. Notice that the past tense in in the prefective; the question is whether this action was completed, and the answer is that a decision was made <u>not to do</u> it.

22.

Well I don't have to do that.
—**I need to buy the new textbook.**
—**Well I don't have to. I already bought [it].**

Nothing very new here. Don't worry about the genitive in the italicized model sentence for now.

23.

[I] don't need to do that.
—**You need to buy a new raincoat.**
—**I don't need to, because I like my old one.**

Here the trick is is to come up with logical reasons why you don't need to do whatever is being mentioned. Don't try and be too creative, just provide a logical reason.

Natasha told me that a young man came by [to see me].

4.7▸

24.

Does Boris have the magazine now?

Victor brought the magazine to Boris	Boris has the magazine now.
Victor brought the magazine to Boris	Boris doesn't have the magazine now.

Exercises 24, 25, 26 deal with another characteristic of aspect—the use of the imperfective to indicate the negation of a result.

The imperfective statement implies that the action is no longer in effect. "He brought it, but it is not where he brought it to." "He got the book at the library, but he doesn't have it anymore [the book must be back at the library.]" "She left the money at home, but it isn't there." "Ira took her shoes to be repaired, but she has them back now."Each one of these incidences should be carefully read and understood.

The perfective shows that the result is still in force. "He brought the dictionary to Sveta, and she still has it." and so on.

25.

Is Victor at Marina's now?

Victor dropped by Marina's	Victor is now at Marina's
Victor dropped by Marina's	Victor was at Marina's, but left.

This exercise practices the same concept as 24, but with verbs of motion.

26.

I took... I took.
Where did you get that tie?
—**Where did you get that tie?**
—**I borrowed it from my brother.**

This exercise requires you to understand the context and provide an answer using the correct aspect.

27.

More practice with **сам**, this time in the dative case and combined with aspect practice.

Урок 5 Устные упражнения

5.2▶

1.

Where is XXX sold
—**Tell me please, where is meat sold?**
—**In the meat department.**
—**Thank you.**

This exercise provides more practice with the prepositional case (all are your everyday garden variety masc. sing e.g. в рыбном отделе, except 5 and seven which are substantived adjectives. They will be в булочной, в кондитерской— in the bakery, in the pastry shop). You must learn this vocabulary. The foods are: cheese, herring (an important food in Russian culture), chocolate, cognac, bread, mandarin oranges, cake, lettuce (in the right context also 'salad'), sour cream, caviar, mineral water, tea. The departments are: dairy, fish, pastry, wine, bakery, "Vegetables&Fruits", pastry shop, vegetable, dairy, fish, "Waters&Juices", dry goods.

Note the verb form. It is reflexive and agrees in number with the grammatical subject (in these sentences the thing being sold). This is one of the two constructions used for impersonal or passive expressions in this chapter. Since the verb agrees with the thing being sold, be careful that you say for #6: Где продаются мадарины?.

2.

Where can you buy ...
—**Where can you buy a tie around here?**
—**In the department store, in the men's department [haberdashery is not a common word for most Americans, so we'll use men's department instead, but next time you're in a fancy men's clothes store you might see the word haberdashery—take a look]**
—**Thank you.**

This exercise gives us still more practice with the vocabulary of purchases, the prepositional case and the expression можно.
The words are (and you must learn them): perfume (note that it is plural in Russian, though it does make any difference here), watch, scarf from Pavlov, cigarettes, flowers, toys, posters, records, fabric, stamps and envelopes, salt. The places are (and, again, you must learn them): the store "Perfume", the jewlery store "Diamond", the store "Russian souvenir", the kiosk [a small booth on the street] "Tobacco", the store "Flowers", "Children's World", the book store, the store "Melodia", the department store-the department "Fabric", post office (remember it takes на), dry goods store.
You don't have to worry about putting the names of the stores in the right case, they remain in the nominative if preceeded by the word "store" "department" "kiosk" etc... though the words "store" "department" "kiosk" etc... will be in the case required (here in the prepositional).

3.

Yes, they sell souvenirs here.
—**Are souvenirs sold in this store?**
—**Yes, they sell souvenirs here.**

This exercise is challenging in that the dialogue provides two passive constructions in the model, and you must learn them both and understand them both. The first line is similar to the first line of the first exercise. The verb is reflexive and agrees with the grammatical subject. The answer uses a third person plural verb form with no explicit subject and the word that was the subject in the question is now the direct object and thus in the accusative case. For instance in number 2, the English would sound like this: Does

31

this library close at five? Yes, they close the library at five. In Russian it will go like this: Эта библиотека закрывается в пять? Да, закрывают библиотеку в пять.

4.

So where are new books sold?
—**What do they sell in the store "Bukinist"?**
—**They sell old books there.**
—**So where are new books sold?**
—**New books are sold in the book store opposite it.**

This exercise combines both passive constructions and much of the vocabulary from the earlier exercises. Make sure you can put everything in the right form, and don't forget the places that take на (#2).

Some notes. мужская is, due to regressive assimilation, pronounced мушская. "Regressive assimilation" described the phenomenon in Russian phonetics in which the voiced or devoiced quality of consonants in consonant clusters derives from the last consonant. A word final consonant is devoiced. So, in Russian the word хле**б** is pronounced хле**п**, the phrase **в** первый ра**з** is pronounced **ф** первый ра**с**, the word селё**дк**а is pronounced селё**тк**а, the word **вк**усный is pronounced **фк**усный, the word э**кз**амен is pronounced э**гз**амен (all these examples except the last one reflect voiced consonants being devoiced). This is opposite to the situation in English (we pronounce the word ballads-balladz, whereas a Russian would want to say "ballats" and confuse us and make us think they were talking not about Shakespeare, but politics. Be aware that your mispronunciation will cause similar problems)

5.

Give him a record!
—**What do you think I ought to give Sasha [Advise, what best to give to Sasha]**
—**Give Sasha a record**
—**Yeah, you're right, I'll give him a record. [Yes, perhaps, I'll give him a record.]**

This exercise is almost exclusively devoted to a phrase for asking for advice, the imperative of подарить, and practice with the word пожалуй which means "perhaps" but doesn't have the stylistic high tone that "perhaps" does in English. пожалуй is used much more frequently in Russian than "perhaps" is in English so for a good translation into English you often have to have the whole context. The presents suggested are: a ring, perfume, a watch (plural), a box of candies, a tie, a scarf from Pavlov, a tray, a photo album, a nesting doll.

6.

Show me the XXX, please
—**Show me the hat please**
—**Which one, this one?**
—**No, that one over there.**

This exercise contrasts the adjective какой and the demonstrative pronouns этот and тот, and gives some practice putting them in the accusative case. Be careful to match their forms with that of the antecedent. Thus the model is right for all feminine nouns, but for the plural nouns the forms will be какие, эти, те. For the neuter (#5), какое, это, то; for the masculine (#3,6,7, 11), какой, этот, тот. Below is a chart of these words in the accusative (note, the masc. and plural forms given are for inanimate only):

masc.	какой	этот	тот
fem	какую	эту	ту
neuter	какое	это	то
plural	какие	эти	те

7.

Buy me XXX, please...
—**Are you going to the store?**
—**Yes, I need to buy cheese.**
—**I do too [And I need to]. Can you buy me some, too , please. [Buy me, please, cheese]**
—**Cheese? Anything else? [And what else?]**
—**Nothing else.**
—**Okay, I'll buy it.**

This exercise is straight forward in that all you need to do is put the cues in for the things to buy. Be careful to put the words in the accusative — that will affect the sound of only #4 and #5. Notice that the English sentence uses a more complex construction to express a request. Instead of simply saying "buy please" we tend to use "can you buy." Russians use a more direct construction for simple polite requests; you should, too.

8.

Yes, please buy ...
—**Should I buy you some milk?**
—**Yes, please, buy (some)**

Again, we have a simpler Russian construction. Instead of saying convoluted and, for the Russian ear, incomprehensible things like Должен ли я купить вам молоко?, just master this construction. It is made up of the infitive and the right intonation (IC-3). The cues are: "explain how to get to the store", show you the photo album, wrap your purchase, help, write you a receipt, order this children's book, pour tea, wrap this box of candies.
The other half of this exercise is the formation of the imperative. They are all perfective and all indicate a polite request to do something once.

The imperative is formed most characteristically by adding и to the stem (with accompanying consonant mutations). All of the verbs in this exercise except #7 do this. The imperatives are: объясни́те, покажи́те, заверни́те, помоги́те, вы́пишите, закажи́те, нале́йте, заверни́те

9.

I've already gone and got milk.
—**I'm going to the store now. Should I buy you some milk?**
—**No, don't. I've already gone and got milk.**

Here, once again the grammar of the situation is less troublesome than the learning of the phrases. You must learn these phrases and what they mean. This exercise adds a negative imperative (in the imperfective) не покупайте, and the phrase сходить за чем in the past tense. The phrase сходить за takes an instrumental complement so you will have to put these purchases not only in the accusative, but also in the instrumental. Make sure you can do this. The words in this exercise are:

accusative	за + instrumental.	English
хлеб	за хлебом	bread
конфеты	за конфетами	candies
вино	за вином	wine
сок	за соком	juice
яблоки	за яблоками	apples
масло	за маслом	butter
сахар	за сахаром	sugar

сметану	за сметаной	sour cream
чай	за чаем	t e a

сходить , in the phrase сходить за is a perfective verb. If this contradicts your understanding that multidirectional verbs of motion become imperfective when a prefix is added, you are to be congratulated on learning that rule so well. Unfortunately that rule is not airtight, and this verb, when it means "to go and get something" instead of "to get off, disembark, come down" is perfective (These different meanings are a result of the prefix c- having different meanings).

We can see the completion component in the English translation for this exercise: *gone and got*

HOWEVER!!! If this peculiarity did not strike you, then don't fret about it. You must learn these phrases whether or not you understand the grammatical intricacies right now.

10.
Buy it, you'll like it.
—You've never bought this wine?
—No, never bought it.
—Buy it, you'll like it.

This exercise provides practice with the imperfective in the past for an action that never occured, and a perfective imperative as a polite command to do something once.

The pairs and the perfective imperatives are: заходить/зайти-зайди́те, пробовать/попробовать (а -овать verb so be careful to form the correct imperative попро́буйте), покупать/купить-купи́те, смотреть/посмотреть-посмотри́те. All these verbs should be familiar. пробовать is related to the English words "probation," "probe," and means to try.

11.
Advise your friend ...
to try ... (you should know what all these things are)
to buy ... (ditto above)
to see ... (ditto)

This is just practice with the material introduced earlier.

5.4▶

12.
I like ... How much does it cost?
—Can I look at this record?
—Please.
—I like this record? How much does it cost?
—The record costs 62 rubles.

Items and thier cost. Unfortunately, even this recent a book cannot keep up with inflation in Russia, and unless there is a major devaluation very soon, these prices will only be more and more out of date as time passes. For one thing there are no kopecks in circulation, but you still should learn the basic nominative, genitive singular and plural forms. If you don't know your numbers learn them:

100	сто
200	две́сти
300	три́ста
400	четы́реста
500	пятьсо́т
600	шестьсо́т
700	семьсо́т
800	восемьсо́т

900	девятьсо́т
1000	ты́сяча
2000	две ты́сячи
3000	три ты́сячи
4000	четы́ре ты́сячи
5000	пять ты́сяч

The word ты́сяча is a feminine noun that acts like a feminine noun, i.e. it will decline when in the accusative case to ты́сячу, and if preceded by another number in the nominative or accusative case it will be in the genitive singular (for 2,3,4 and compounds ending in those numbers, except 12, 13, 14, of course) or the genitive plural (for 5 and compounds ending in 5).

Another thing to remember here is that the nouns need to be in the accusative in the first phrase, the nominative in the second, and you need to provide the correct pronoun in the second part of that third line.

13.

Play at the cashiers window.
—How much does this scarf cost?
—It costs 554 rubles.
—554 rubles? I'll take it.
—Pay at the cashier's window.

More practice with numbers here. Note (#6) that Russians, like most Europeans, deliminate thousands with a point, and use a comma to set off decimals.

14.

Buy that one, it is tastier than that one.
—Which book should I buy, that one or this?
—Buy that one, it's more interesting.

This exercise introduces and practice the simple comparative degree. Its called the simple comparative not because it is so simple—you have to learn yet another form—but because it isn't the compound form. They seem to come from adjectives, but to call them adjectives is also somewhat misleading since if they were adjectives they would agree with the nouns they modify, would decline and do all those good things that adjectives are wont to do. The simple comparative form doesn't change (so maybe in that way it is simple); it is only used predicatively (you can't put it in front of a noun) and with verbs, so we are better off if we think of these forms as adverbs. In the exercise "more interesting" describes "how is" the book.

You need to learn many comparative forms. Below are the ones from this exercise and all the ones from the written homework. Note the stress, and the consonant mutations. The stress depends on the number of syllables-if the underlying adjective has two syllables then the stress will be on the first of two е́е, otherwise it will be as in the underlying adjective. The regular, full ending is е́е, but there are many frequent forms that are "irregular." (This chart is also in the end of this material under this chapter's written exercises).

Adjective	Comparative	English
свéжий	свежéе	fresh/er
вкýсный	вкуснéе	tasty/ier
красúвый	красúвее	pretty/ier
дешёвый	дешéвле	cheap/er
дорóгой	дорóже	dear/er
слáдкий	слáще	sweet/er

	No mutation, full "ee" ending:	
весёлый	веселéе	happy/ier
бы́стрый	быстрéе	quick/er
мéдленный	мéдленнее	slow/er
свéтлый	светлéе	light/er (bright/er)
тёмный	темнéе	dark/er
трýдный	труднéе	more difficult
вáжный	важнéе	more important
интерéсный	интерéснее	more interesting

	ONE LETTER Mutation:	
дорогóй	дорóже	dear/er, more expensive
грóмкий	грóмче	loud/er
тúхий	тúше	quiet/er
богáтый	богáче	rich/er

	More than one letter mutation	
дешёвый	дешéвле	cheap/er
блúзкий	блúже	close/r
далёкий	дáльше	far/ther
слáдкий	слáще	sweet/er

	From different roots	
хорóший	лýчше	good/better
плохóй	хýже	bad/worse
мáленький	мéньше	small/er
большóй	бóльше	bigg/er

15.

Yes, she sings better.
—Listen to how well she sings!
—Yes, but he sings better than she.

This exercise provides practice with comparatives that are clearly from adverbs, and are adverbs themselves. The adverb from большóй is много (a lot, much; as in I work a lot). The comparative form is бóльше. Other than this all the adverbs should be clear. The verbs should also present no problem. Make sure you know what you are saying.

5.5▶

16.

What would you say, if...
to open
The window is open and you are cold
—Close (perf.) the window, please.

It is winter and your roommate always leaves the window open in the evening.
—**Close (imperf.) the window please.**

You are supposed to provide the correct imperative in these exercises. Contexts that unambiguously require the use of an imperfective or perfective imperative are provided. Your task is to read through and understand the contexts and then provide the correct imperative. This may take some time, so make sure you set aside a block of time to work on these.

17.

Please write neatly...

(more slowly, more quickly, in more detail, more attentively, louder)
—**Write an announcement.**
—**Okay, I will.**
—**Please write neatly.**

This little dialogue is packed with things. In the first place note that the comparative is used in this very natural sounding Russian, but it is not well translated with the comparative in English. The comparative here adds emphasis. As to emphasis, this dialogue also illustrates the use of the imperfective imperative to point out how something is to be done. Here we have a polite request in the perfective followed by a imperative in the imperfective.

You will need to make the choice as far as adverbs are concerned, so make sure you understand the situation. Spend some time going through this and prepare it.

18.

Prepare dialogues:

You've got some heavy bags in your arms. You ask your friend to open the car door. She says she will right away, but you want her to do it sooner.
—**Open the car door please.**
—**Just a minute, I'll open it right away.**
—**Open it, open it. I've got heavy bags.**

This exercise asks you to understand situations where one would encounter the use of the imperfective imperative to hurry some action that is delayed. You need to provide the lines for the dialogues.

5.6▶

19.

Don't wait
—**Should I (we) wait for you?**
—**No, don't wait. You don't need to.**

For this dialogue you need to know the imperfective so that you can form an imperfective imperative in a negative command (a command NOT to do something). The imperfectives are: закрыва́ть, расска́зывать, покупа́ть, завора́чивать, надева́ть, помога́ть.

20

Don't buy it, I already bought it.
—**I'll go buy some bread.**
—**Don't buy it, I've already bought it.**

Here again the imperative is in the imperfective because the command is negative. The imperfectives are: включа́ть, открыва́ть, звони́ть, плати́ть, закрыва́ть, отдава́ть, смотре́ть, спра́шивать. Make sure you know what the dialogues you are constructing mean.

21.

Make dialogues
Your friend wants to buy a nesting doll. You advise him not to because it is very expensive.
—I want to buy this nesting doll.
—Don't buy it. It's very expensive.

This is more practice with the imperfective imperative in negative commands. As in earlier exercises, this one requires that you understand the situation presented and then produce an appropriate dialogue. Again, it may take a while so give yourself some time.

22.

Watch out, don't be late.
—The exam starts at eight o'clock sharp. Don't be late!

Here we have a negative command, but the perfective. This is a result of a context in which the negative command is an effort to prevent an undersired result such as, in this example missing the beginning of an exam or waking a child or missing a flight or forgetting something important. The commands here are: don't be late, don't oversleep, don't wake, don't forget.

5.7►

> **But in the doors to the store there were so many people that it was impossible to get in.**

23.

You can't get in! You mustn't come in!

The word нельзя means different things depending on the aspect of the infinitive used. A perfective infinitve indicates that the action cannot be done (though there may be no prohibition against it). An imperfective infinitive with нельзя indicates a prohibition against the action. You need to understand the contexts provided and choose the correct aspect. Again, you need to go through these contexts and understand them as you prepare for class.

24.

Continue

—Can you open this door?	—Can you open this door?
—No, this door can't be opened.	—No, I can't open it.
—why not?	—Why not?
—Because there's a rehearsal going on there.	—Because I don't have the key.

Here you need to offer reasons that would be appropriate to the use of the aspect given. Take your time and do these thoroughly.

6.2▶

1

On the floor lies a large rug.
He lay the model on the floor
---

1. This exercise highlights the spatial meaning of the intransitive verbs of postion. Fill in the blanks with the correct verbs.

2.

Lay the book on the shelf.   Let the book lie on the shelf.

As with the English verbs "to lie[to be in a lying position]" and "to lay," the Russian verbs "лежать[its perfective is formed by adding the prefix по-, and it means to be lying down for a short time; it is not introduced here]" and "класть-положить" are easy to confuse and must be carefully learned and extensively practiced.

The English verb "to lay" is transitive: hens lay eggs, they don't lie them. This contrast between intransitive and transitive verbs, i.e. verbs of position and verbs of positioning is found in four common sets in Russian — to be standing (стоять) vs. to place in a standing position (ставить/поставить), to be in a lying position (лежать) vs. to place in a lying position (класть/положить [this is a so called suppletive pair, i.e. the imperfective and perfective are formed from different roots, further complicating matters]), to be hanging (висеть) vs. to hang up (вешать/повесить), to be in a sitting positon (сидеть) vs. to seat someone (сажать/посадить).

Notice here that since placing things implies movement the destinations (the wall, a vase, a table, the closet, pocket, refrigerator, armchair) in the examples are designated by **в** or **на** plus the accusative (and questions about destination with these verbs will use, of course, **куда**). The places in the continuations (which you are supposed to provide) will be in the prepositional since these are positions not destinations.

The word **пусть** introduces what is called the third person imperative. It is fairly simple to use. Use the word **пусть** plus the conjugated form of the verb.

You must learn these verbs, how they are conjugated and how they are used in order to speak Russian correctly. This exercise (#2) contrasts the transitive and intransitive verbs.

3.

—**Why is the vase standing on the window (sill)?   Who put the vase on the window?**
—**I don't know who put it there.   I didn't (put it there).**
—**Put it in its place.**

In addition to contrasting the transitive and intransive verbs, this exercise also contrasts the use of prepositional and accusative after **в** or **на** to indicate the place. The dialogue shows that for verbs of position (the intransitive ones) the place where the objects are located is indicated by **в** or **на** plus the prepostional: Почему ваза стоит <u>на окне</u>? For verbs of placing and putting (the transitive ones), the place that the objects are put is indicated by **в** or **на** plus the accusative case: Кто поставил её <u>на окно</u>?

4.

—**Where's your dictionary at? [where lies your dictionary?]**
—**I don't remember where I put it yesterday.   Usually its lying on the shelf.**
—**Well, its not here.   Maybe you put it in the cabinet?**
—**Maybe, have a look.**

Again, the idea that the verbs of position deal with place [thus the question **Где** у тебя лежит словарь? and the prepositional case: Он обычно лежит **на полке**.], is contrasted with verbs of positioning [thus Я не помню **куда** я положила его вчера, and Может быть, ты положила его **в шкаф**?].

It is also worth noting the use of the possessive phrase "Где **у тебя** лежит словарь?" This phrase conveys the sense of "where do you usually store your dictionary." This is not the point being practiced here, just learn the phrase and try to use it.

The exercise also includes a very common imperative ("have a look" or "take a look").

6.3▶

6.
—**I like macaroni and cheese, how about you?**
—**Macaroni and cheese, yeah, its pretty good.**

This exercise practices some of the more common lexical items you will need to talk about food. It also requires you to recall the instrumental plural forms. Nouns that end in -а/я in the nominative singular will take -ой/ей or -ёй(if end stressed) in the instrumental singular. Neuter nouns in -е or -о and masculine nouns that end in a consonant (i.e. they have a zero [ø] ending) in the nominative will take -ом or -ем or sometimes even -ём in the instrumental singular. Plural nouns add -ами in the instrumental.

This exercise also provides some practice with the fourth intonational construction, a question started with "**а**".

7.
—**Want to try some mushroom pie?**
—**Mushroom pie? I'd love to!**

This exercise provides some more practice with food words and the instrumental and includes a very common and useful phrase for expressing strong consent that also has an instrumental form: "с удовольствием".

It also provides practice with the verbs "**хотеть**" and "**попробовать**"

8.
—**Have you tried this salad yet? Try it, it's really good.**
—**Thanks. Wow, you're right, it really is good.**

This exercise practices the imperative of "**попробовать**" (it is a -**ова** verb, so its imperative is "**попро́буй(те)**") This is a very useful imperative—learn it and use it.

This exercise also practices the polite question formula with a the negative word "**не**".

Further, the exercise underscores the use of the word "**вкусно**" for describing "good" food.

9.
—**Have some salad.**
—**What's it got in it?**
—**It's fish salad.**
—**No, thanks. I don't like fish salad.**

—**Have some borshch.**
—**What's it got in it?**
—**Borshch with sour cream.**
—**No, thanks. I don't like borshch with sour cream.**

This exercise provides more practice with food words and the instrumental case, and provides simple formulas for offering someone something to eat and politely refusing something offered to eat.

6.4▶
Exercises   11-14

These exercises illustrate the usage of the particles -**нибудь** and -**то**. These particles can be added to pronouns, adjectives and adverbs that can be interrogatives (когда, где, etc...). In this lesson we will try to master their use with что and кто only, though in all their inflected forms. Only the pronoun part will change if the syntax requires.

Since these two particles don't have convenient one-to-one English equivalents the proper use of these particles is a difficult point, and the waters are often muddied by explanations that imply that -**нибудь** corresponds to "any-" (anything, anybody, etc...) and that -**то** corresponds to "some-" (something, anything, etc...). In our attempts to render the Russian into good English it seems that this rule often works. This "rule" however is not a good predictor, i.e. if you would use "anything" in a natural English sentence, there is no guarantee that -**нибудь** would work. Sometimes, in fact it is simply a counter predictor. For instance, neither of these particle is ever used in negative sentences in Russian, such as "I don't want <u>anything</u>."

Another problem is that "any-" and "some-" are often nearly interchangeable in English (e.g. "Did he buy anything?"≈"Did he buy something?"). In Russian -**то** and -**нибудь** are never interchangeable, and "Did he buy anything?" and "Did he buy something?" would both have to be rendered **Он что-нибудь купил?**

While we are getting used to using these particles we can use a rule of thumb:

1. with Imperatives (including the third person 'imperatives': **пусть/пускай**) and Questions, -**нибудь** will usually be the right choice.

2. For past tense (except questions) -**то** will usually be the right choice.

In other contexts use -**то** for known but not named things, and -**нибудь** to express unknown elements.

A possible mnemonic device: **I**(mperative)**QU**(estion)=н**И**б**У**дь. Pas**T**=**T**о.

It might help to examine the morphology of -**нибудь**. We can see that there is some form (it looks like the imperative) from the verb **быть** in the particle. If we imagine that the particle -**нибудь** conveys the sense of "what (who, when, etc…) -ever it might **be**" we can come close to the idea of the what -**нибудь** means. The particle -**то** can, perhaps also be understood if the sense of the indicative pronoun **то** is remembered. It is used to indicate something that is known to exist, but is not specified.

11.
—**Can you give me something [whatever it might be] to eat, please?**
—**What do you want?**
—**It doesn't matter, anything [whatever it might be].**

The main point in this exercise illustrates the use of the particle -**нибудь**. In both the instances in the Russian example the particle -**нибудь** indicates that the speaker doesn't care what it is that they get to get, just that they get something.

12.
—**What are they eating?**
—**I don't know, but something really good.**

This exercise illustrates the use of the particle -**то**. Since it is clear that the people are eating, even though we don't know what they are eating we know that a dish exists, therefore, -**то** is used.

13.
—**What is he telling about?**
—**I don't know, but probably about something interesting.**

Again, we don't know what it is that is being talked about, but that there is a story being related we don't doubt. Therefore we use the particle -**то**.

14.
—**Did anyone** [whoever it might be] **come by to see me?**
—**Yeah, someone did come by.**
—**Who?**
—**I don't know who it was.**

Here we have a combination of both particles. In the question it isn't known whether or not there were any visitors or not so -**нибудь** is naturally used. In the answer it is known that there was a visitor, but who it was is unknown so -**то** is used.

6.5▶

Exercises 16,17&18. These exercises cover the use of the first person ("Let's"<Let us [do something]) and third person (Let him, her, them [do something]) imperatives . See PT-90, ex. 22.

The first person imperative is formed by the word **давай(те)** and the "we" form of the future. If the context requires the imperfective the word **будем** is optional and most often omitted. All the examples here use the plural/polite form. [If the "us" in "Let us" refers to just two people "you and I" and the "you" is "**ты**" then **давай** is used. If the "us" refers to either more than two people or the "you" is "**вы**" then **давайте** is used.] The choice of aspect for the future form depends on the context. In 16&17 all the contexts imply a single action to be completed once, therefore the perfective future is used. In 18 the imperfective future is used (**будем** is omitted, so it looks just as if the imperfective infinitive were being used, but it is a good idea to understand that it is a future form with **будем** understood). Since the imperfective is used here we can assume that it is not the intention of the speaker to emphasize the completion of a single action. The speaker conveys that it is the action itself that is important here, not the completion per se.

The third person imperative (16&17 only) is formed by the word **пусть** followed by the person or persons in the nominative and verb in the present or future (either aspect). The aspect, again, depends on the context; all the examples here use the perfective future because the contexts imply a single completed action.

Notice that in ex. 16 the imperfective is used after **не хочу**.

16.
(p. 194) Let's set the table
—**I don't want to set the table. Have Ira set it.**

17.
-**Why don't we buy the champagne, and Boris'll buy the cake.**
—**No, let Boris buy the champagne and we'll buy the cake.**

18.
What do you want to do now?
—**Let's have dinner.**
—**Ok, sound's great [we have agreed]!**

19.

Here we practice the first person imperative some more and also practice using the verb **предлагать**, a very handy verb.

—I say we make a toast in honor of Irina
—Ok, let's drink to Irina.

—I say we dance.
—Ok, let's dance.

20.

More practice with the first person imperative (notice that the **давай** form is used so we know that there are only two people and that the "you" is "**ты**"). We also practice the expression of mild desire or lack thereof rendered in the impersonal construction "**кому (не) хочется** что делать".

Furthermore, the very important short form adjective **сыт, сыта, сыты** is covered.

—Let's have another pastry.
—No, I don't really feel like it. I'm already full.

6.6▶
22.

These dialogues help reinforce the first person singular forms of "to eat" and "to drink." They also reinforce the idea that the imperfective future is fine in a first person imperative if the intention of the speaker is to simply state the action, not emphasize any result or completion of the action.

Notice also that the direct object in the third line is the first word of the sentence. This reflects the use of the theme and rheme in Russian word order.

Finally, this exercise repeats the verb "**предлагать/предложить**" in a different context.

—Let's have some meat	—Let's drink vodka
—I don't eat meat.	—I don't drink vodka
—What about fish?	—How about beer.
—I don't eat fish either.	—I don't drink beer either
—What can I offer you, then?	—What can I offer you then?

23.

Here we practice the informal "you" form of "to eat" and repeat the construction "кому (не) хочется что делать". This time we're adding a verb (in the imperfective).
—How come you're not eating?
—I don't know. I don't feel like eating.

24.

This exercise reviews and recycles the time telling material (you see, you didn't have to know it perfectly last time, but we need all the practice we can get, so try and get it this time). It also brings in the use of the word "**пора**" and the imperfective infinitive.
—What time is it?
—Eight o'clock
—Really, it's already eight? It's time to sit down to eat.

25.

Now, in addition to time, we're adding a "subject" to the "**пора**" statement. The logical subject, better described as the "agent", is here in the dative. Since it is also not a nominative construction in English, "it is time for us, her, John..." this is not a particularly difficult point. Notice the imperfective again.

—It's already six am.; it's time for us to get up

26.

This exercise reviews some vocabulary and the use of the perfective in a question in the past to emphasize that something hasn't been done yet, followed by the construction **пора** with the imperfective. The last sentence is in the perfective future since the speaker is emphasizing one completed act [but here all you need to do is repeat the condition supplied].

—You aren't dressed yet?[you haven't got dressed yet?] It's time you got dressed. We'll be late for the theater.

6.7▶

Ex. 27, 28, 29

These all practice and reinforce the use of the constructions "**Мы с ...**" "**Вы с ...**" and "**Они с ...**". These constructions arc used instead of "**Я и ..**" "**Ты/вы и ...**" and "**он/она/они и ...**" which our North American, Anglo speaking tongues crave to pronounce. Learn to use this construction and you will sound authentic!

The exercises further practice the use of the perfective past and future and the "**пора**" plus imperfective infinitive construction.

27.
—Who arrived first, you and Sasha?
—Yeah, Sasha and I arrived first?

28.
—Who's going to buy the present?
—Irina and I will buy the gift.
—And who'll buy the flowers.
—And you and Oleg buy the flowers, please.

29.
—Is it already time to leave?
—Yup, it's time for Sasha and me to leave.

31.

This exercises illustrates the use of an imperfective imperative for strong requests or invitiation. Use the cues offered at the beginning of the exercise to complete the sentences.

—It's my birthday. Come over!

32.
This is a poem that you are to complete. The words mean— "didn't find" "aren't coming", "finished off[eating]", "invited", "bit off", "pie."

7.2▶

1.

—**What course did Linda choose?**
—**A course on the history of the theater.**
—**Really? I picked that course, too.**

The grammar here is pretty straightforward. We have the past of a bunch of verbs: to buy, to go, to write, to take [a test], to like. But mostly we are practicing the use of **по**. This preposition is tough because it is used in many contexts that in English use various prepositional clauses, and sometimes just adjective-noun clauses without a preposition. We need to get used to using **по** in a wide variety of contexts, and some are practiced here.

In all these instances, and most always, **по** governs the dative case. We already know the use of this construction in the phrases "Кто он по специальности" and "Он специалист по русскому языку." If you don't remember that exercise, go back and have a look, p. 10. Try and go through all the examples. In English we can render the phrase "A Russian course" as "a course in Russian". The only equivalent Russian construction is "**курс по русскому языку**."

The samples show various uses of **по** in different instances: 1.an album (cocktail table art book) **on** the art of the 20th cent., or, A 20th century Russian art album 2.a film **based on** Tolstoy's novel <u>War and Peace</u>. 3. A test **in** Russian.or A Russian test   4.An exam **on** the history of the Fine Arts. or A history of the fine arts exam. 5. The section of the museum **devoted to** the history of film.

We are also practicing the use of **тоже**. Notice that **тоже** is used here because it is "Linda did something, and somebody else did the same thing." That is, the subject is different, the action is the same.

If you don't remember the forms for the dative, you might refer to this chart, but you will be expected to know these endings. Also see the explanation after chapter one, dialogue 15, above:

First declension (masculine nouns in a consonant and neuter nouns in a basic [o], that is, o, ё, e.) The ending is basic [u], that is either -**у**,or -**ю**. For example: **фильму, роману, искусству**	For second declension nouns (those ending in basic [a], that is, -a -я) the ending is -**е**. For example: **книге, Ване** **HOWEVER!** Feminines in -**ия** have -**ии** in the dative, e.g. по **истории**	For third declension nouns (feminine nouns in -ь), the dative ending is -**и,** e.g. по **специальности**	For plural nouns, the ending in the dative is (in basic sounds)[-am], i.e. -**ам**, -**ям**. For example: по **вопросам**
For adjectives modifying masculine or neuter nouns: -**ому/-ему**	For adjectives modifying feminine nouns: -**ой/ей**		For adjectives modifying plural nouns: -**ым/-им**

2.

—**What show did Linda see?**
—**A show based on Schvartz' play "The Dragon."**
—**Did she like the show?**
—**Yes, she liked it very much.**

In this model we find the preposition **по** used to express what in English is rendered by "based on" as in number 2 of the first exercise. Again, there is little new grammar; you just need to get used to the various contexts. All of these examples illustrate the "based on..." use.

3.
—**What did you do yesterday?**
—**We went to an exhibition.**
—**Which one?**
—**To an exhibition of abstrationists.**
—**Is it worth seeing?**
—**Yes, I recommend going.**

There are no big grammar points to mention here. Note that the noun **выставка** takes **на**, and that the question Which one? is not just **какая** but **на какую?** since it is in response to "We went <u>to an exhibition</u>." If you are rusty on the formation of the genitive plural, this exercise gives you some practice (in 1,3,4,5 the adjectives all take the genitive plural **-ых** ending). In the others the adjectives take the singular masculine/neuter **-ого**. The plural nouns here all take the **-ов** ending. The others take the masculine/neuter **-а**. See the tables on pp. 371-2 if you need to brush up. The cues mean: 1. young artists, 2. old Russian art, 3. French artists 4. American modernists 5. Moscow Conceptualists 6. Italian Renaissance.

You might wonder what this **сходить** verb is doing here. If you compare the constructions with "**советовать**" (see dialogue 2, p. 171) that we've had earlier, you will notice that they seem to take a perfective "advice me what to buy." If that's so, then can it be true that **сходить** is a perfective verb even though we have this impression that prefixed indeterminate verbs of motion are imperfective? Yes, it is true — see PT-102. **сходить** is in fact a perfective verb and it is used in contexts like this one where one should "go and see" something (a movie, a play, an exhibition). That it is perfective is reviewed and built on in lesson 10. For now you just have to remember the construction "**советую сходить**" and what it means.

4.
—**Do you know when the Theater Poster Exhibition is open.**
—**The Theater Poster Exhibition? Yeah. From 11 to 5.**
—**Is it going to be up for much longer?**
—**Not, it closes in a week.**

Here we have some more practice with the genitive, impersonal constructions ("it closes") and time expressions. We also get more practice with the very appropriate construction for an inquiry to solicit information, **Вы не знаете**. Practice this phrase and sound like a native. The cues are: 1. contemporary painting (it's feminine 3rd declension, so the genitive will be **современной живописи**), 2. icons (it's feminine so the genitive plural will be **икон**). The other cues are pretty obvious, I hope.

5.
—**Do you know where the film "The Blonde Around the Corner" is showing?**
—**"The Blonde Around the Corner" is showing at the cinema theatre "Kosmos".**
—**And what's showing at the "Rossia"**
—**Don't know.**

Here we're practicing the **Вы не знаете** construction, and the phrase **идёт фильм**.

46

7.3►

6.

—Shall we go to the ballet "Swan Lake" today?
—Where?
—To the Bolshoi.
—But its really hard to get in there.
—I already got tickets
—How, where?
—Doesn't matter (It's not important), shall we go?
—Of course, let's go.

This exercise offers more practice with the first person imperative (notice that the form пойдём is used without давайте, this is fine). It also practices the phrase, "I already got tickets" a handy thing to be able to say; try using it with other things you might get.

7.

—Do you know that an exhibition of antique bronzes has opened?
—Yes, I heard. They say it is really interesting.
—Let's go.
—Let's.

This exercise practices a new "Do you know" phrase, without the "не" that is used not to ask for information, but to introduce the statement of information (rhetorically). It also helps us work on the handy phrase "They say" to pass on second hand infomation. Again we have the verb "сходить" in the sense of "go and see." The cues are: 1. in the neighboring cinema a new comedy is showing. 2. in the Drama Theater there's a new show. 3. In the club a new rock group is performing. 4. there's a free concert in the park today. 5. a new gallery has opened.

8.

—I've never been in Petersburg.
—If you're ever in Petersburg, you must go to the Hermitage and the Russian Museum.

Here we practice a negative construction "никогда не был", please learn it [if you don't, I'll have to stop saying please]. Also learn to pronounce Petersburg in Russian, anyone who doesn't ... Anyway...

Notice that the English construction "If you're ever in ..." uses a present construction and the word "ever." In the Russian it is a future construction that we would like to translate "If you will be in Petersburg." The context here, doesn't let us translate it this way. [the Russian could also have когда-нибудь]. And then we have more practice with the verb сходить. The cues are all pretty clear; read them and be sure you can put all the place names in the prepositional and accusative (the cities are in the prepositional, the places to see in the cities are in the accusative [verbs of motion]—if you don't know why find out, this is a basic point). Notice also that Афины is a plural noun, strange but true, so it will be in the prepositional plural "в Афинах."

7.4►

10.

—An artist is a person who paints pictures.

This exercises asks you to describe professions. Match the professions in the left column with the activities that best describe what they do in the right column. Construct a sentence according to the model. You'll get practice conjugating verbs and using который in the nominative case. You must learn these verbs that you might not know: выступать(выступа́й+) на сцене (to perform on stage), сочинят (сочиняй+)—to compose (cf. сочинение—composition), ставить(стави+) спектакли—to put on shows (plays). Make sure you know the words стихи, пьесы. Also note the phrase писать иконы. This is the correct way to say "paint" when something artistic is implied—to "write" icons.

11.

a.—I was at the exhibition that you were telling me about.
b.—I went to the theater with a friend that arrived not long ago.
c.—I'm talking about the actors, that play in that show.

These three exercises give us some practice using **который** clauses. If you are not yet comfortable with these clauses, these may take some time. Work through the examples slowly, and check them below. **Который** is called a "relative pronoun." It is relative because it derives its meaning from its antecedent, and thus **который** can and will change its number and gender depending on its antecedent. (Personal pronouns derive their meaning from their referents so their gender and number are fixed always and forever). **Который** clauses provide added information about some noun in the main clause. This is not that hard. We just need to understand that the phrase "that you recommended seeing" isn't a complete thought until we add "I was at the exhibition" in front. The Russian is complicated, however, by the fact that **который**, like all Russian pronouns, declines. The basic rule is: **который** takes number and gender from its antecedent and case from the function it performs in the subordinate clause. You must gain facility with **который** clauses in this course, so make sure you understand what is happening in these sentences.

a1. Я была на выставке, которую вы советовали посмотреть. (I was at the exhibition that you recommended seeing)

2. Я была на выставке, которая находится на набережной Невы.(I was at the exhibition that's located on the Neva embankment)

3. Я была на выставке, на которой есть работы молодых художников. (I was at the exhibition where works of young artists are at [at which there are works of young artists].)

4. [same construction as 3]

5. , которая открылась недавно.

б.1. Я ходила в театр с другом, о котором я уже рассказывала вам. [I went to the theater with the friend that I was telling you about.]

2. ..., который живёт в соседнем доме. [that lives in the house next door]

3. ..., с которым я уже вас познакомил. [that I introduced you to.]

4. ..., которого я знаю с детсва. [... that I've known since childhood.]

в. 1. Я говорю об актёрах, с которыми я недавно познакомился. [whom I met not long ago]

2. ..., которых все знают. [whom everyone knows]

3. ..., о которых я читал в журнале «Театр». [about whom I read in the magazine "Theater"]

4. ..., которым предложили поехать на гастроли в США. [who were offered the chance to go on tour in the US.]

5. ..., которые работают в Малом театре.[who work in the Maly theater]

12.

—Did you go to the exhibition?
—[To] which one?
—[The one] that opened recently.
—I went.
—Well, how was it? What was your impression?
—I really liked it.

This is more practice with **который** clauses and a new word **впечатление**. Learn it, love it, use it — at least in the phrase here. Also more practice with the verb

нравиться. All the **который** clauses will be in the nominative case, but that should be self evident from the cues in parentheses.

7.5▶

14.
a.—Did you choose the course on the history of theater?
—Yes, and I'm very satisfied with the course.
b—Did you choose the course on the history of theater?
—Yes, but I'm not satisfied with the course.

This exercise practices the short form adjective **доволен-довольна.** Its dictionary meaning is "to be satisfied/happy with" and it governs the instrumental [a fortunate coincidence with the English construction **EXCEPT** - that **доволен** takes the instrumental without a preposition!]. All the questions use a **по** construction, and you need to answer that you are satisfied or not with the thing in question. Make sure you can form the instrumentals of the words in italics: новым преподавателем, новой программой, новым учебником (new textbook), результатами.

15.
—What's with you? What are you unhappy about [with what are you dissatisfied]?
—Not what, but who. I'm unhappy with myself. [I'm disappointed in myself]

Note the construction for asking somebody what the matter is. In English we can say, "What's with you" in some cases but not all that we can use "**Что с тобой**" in Russian.

This exericise also offers some practice with the instrumental of the personal pronouns and the interrogatives-собой, им, ей, ими, вами, тобой, собой.

16.
—So how did you find the show?
—I'm glad I went.[I am satisfied with the fact, that I went to this show]
—I'm really satisfied, too. I especially liked the acting.

More practice with the **доволен** construction, but we're making it a little more complex. Just as we use a compound structure to express "before/after something happened(i.e. with verbs)" до[после] того, как он пошел..., and перед тем, как она придёт..., to expresses sastisfaction with an action we use a compound structure: доволен тем, что ...

Note the very laconic dative construction for asking somebody what they thought. This is a very conversational and handy construction to learn. Practice these phrases and make them yours.

You might also notice that the verb of motion here is **пошёл.** This is a perfectly natural Russian sentence, and it means little more than "went." The idea of being satisfied and a perfective verb points to the result of the going. Since there is no temporal or spatial meaning intended we find the form пойти is used. We might imagine that the perfective here adds a sense that in English is conveyed by the words "ended up going."

17.
—Are we having play rehearsal tomorrow?
—Yes, why?
—Then this evening I'm going to work on my lines. [study my role]
—You want to learn your part in an evening.
—I'll give it a try.

This exercise is meant to give you practice contrasting the perfective and imperfective of the verb pair **учить/выучить.** You need to match the activities offered to the things from the list of things to be learned at the beginning of the exercise.

Notice the use of **а что?** where we would use a "why?" in English to request additional information after answering a question. This is an important phrase to learn. It can be added after any answer, but can also sound a bit rude in the wrong place.

7.6▶

18.

—What do you think of this novel?
—In my view, it is the most interesting novel.

Besides providing you with more ammunition to solicit someone's opinion and express your own, we work on using the superlative construction **самый**...The superlative is formed by **самый**... plus the adjective.

You also get to polish up your control of the prepositonal case, and practice another way to say "I think". number 6 is "expressive picture" and 7 is "elegant sculpture."

19.

—I think [it seems to me], that this is the most interesting picture in this exhibition.
—Yes, I agree. It is the best of all. It's much more interesting than the other pictures.

Practice with the short form adjective **согласен**, and some more superlatives. We see here, and we will learn to use, the construction "best of all" as another way to express a superlative degree. It is formed by the simple comparative form plus the word **всех** ("of all").

Also get used to using **намного** [and **гораздо**] and the simple comparative to express "much more [interesting, pretty, smart]. The "than" in this construction is expressed here by the genitive right after the adjective. [you may recall, or may not, that you can also use чем plus the nominative to express this, learn the genitive construction here].

Note the handy construction "**мне кажется**"

20.

—Did you like the show?
—No, not very much, although that's my favorite director.
—But it isn't a bad show.
—No, but he has better things.

More practice with the superlative, this one "my most favoritest" you must learn. Also learn the handy word **хотя** "although".

Лучшие here is used as a comparative adjective. Note that it agrees in number with the word **вещи** "things."

7.7▶

22.

—Do you happen to know who founded Moscow university?
—Of course I know. Moscow university was founded by Lomonosov.

This exercise illustrates the use of past passive short form verbal adjectives. Repeat, you do not have to learn the rules of formation of these things yet, but you do need to know what they mean. And the eleven different short form past passive short form verbal adjectives here are worth remembering.

Note that in number 3 the last name Prokofiev, like Lomonosov, and, for that matter all Russian masculine last names in **-ов**, **-ев** or **-ин** (Ломоносов, Бунин, etc...) take an adjective-looking form in the instrumental—**Проковьевым**. In numbers 2 and 6, the last names decline like adjectives, so there's nothing surprising in **Толстым** and **Станисла́вским**. In 4 **Маршак** becomes **Маршако́м**.

поста́влен — поставить

напи́сан—написать

переведён-переведена́/ы́—перевести

постро́ен—построить

со́здан—создать

откры́т—открыть

нарисо́ван—нарисовать

сде́лан—сделать

со́бран—собрать

организо́ван—организовать

осно́ван—основать

решён—решить

про́дан—продать

Work through this exercise slowly.

23.

—Who's this picture painted by?

—Who painted this picture? My brother.

The first line underscores the use of the instrumental to ask "by whom" something "was done".

The second line stresses the underlying verb, using an active construction.

24.

—What do you think, is this museum ever going to be open?

—I'm sure they'll open it soon.

This exericise constrasts the passive construction with a past passive verbal adjective and a passive impersonal construction using the third person plural form of the underlying verb without an explicit subject. You can find other participles in the reading selections. See commentary 3 on pg. 37 for instance

8.2▶

1.
—**Why isn't Linda here today**
—**She's sick.**
—**What's wrong with her?**
—**She's got the flu.**

This exercise illustrates and practices the use of the genitive for the expression of the absense of something or someone. If this is news for you, you should learn that the genitive case is used when someone or something "was not," "is not," or "will not be" (somewhere). The constructions are: Её не было, её нет, её не будет. This is an impersonal construction so do not be tempted to use any other form for the verbs except those listed.

The only tricky example is 7 because Шеррел will not change since it is a foreign feminine name. The verb болеть is conjugated here in one form only, so that is no problem

2.
—**Did you happen to see Sergei?**
—**No, he came down with something yesterday [he got sick yesterday].**
He's not going to be here today.

More practice with the genitive to express absence. Number 9, Мэри, will be the same in accusative (see above), but of course the pronoun will change for the second part of the sentence.

3.
—**I was told [they told me], that you got sick. How do you feel?**
—**I was in a bad way yesterday.**
—**How about today?**
—**Today I'm a lot better.**

Some practice with the impersonal construction (they told me), plus practice conjugating and using чувствовать себя (note that the first в is not pronounced). Then some "I was sick" practice, and repitition of **гораздо** (learn this word; use it; make it yours!!!)

4.
—**You look pretty bad.**
—**Yeah, for some reason I feel sick.**
—**You need to work less.**
—**You're probably right.**

Just some practice with some handy phrases, learn them, love them, use them.

5.
—**I feel cold.**
—**But it's not cold in here. You haven't come down with something, have you?**
—**I don't know, maybe.**

States of being and the dative case. This is not new material, but now you must make it active if it is not yet so. The dative of **ребёнок** is **ребёнку**.

6.
—**Where's Sergei? I haven't seen him for a long time.**
—**He's sick.**
—**Has he been sick for a long time?**
—**Yeah, three days.**

Practice with the short form adjective **болен** and verb **болеть**, and some excellect review of the time expression that can be either with the word "for" or without it in English, but must be **without** a preposition in Russian. Note that неделя will become неделю here.

7.
—**Was Pavel with you on the excursion?**
—**No, he was sick then.**
—**How does he feel now.**
—**Fine, he's healthy now.**

Again, there is really no new grammar to be introduced here, but you need to get used to using the correct past forms for **был(а)** and the verbs. We do have one new short form adjective here **здоро́в(а)**. Don't neglect your pronunciation here. The masculine form, **здоро́в** will end in a devoiced v = [f] sound, but the feminine will have a fully voiced v.

8.3▶
8.
—**Are you coming with us to the movies?**
—**No, I feel sick.**
—**What's wrong?**
—**I have a headache.**
Nothing new but vocabulary to introduce here. Good sentences, and learn the parts of the body. If you don't know the parts of the body, review the words in the vocabulary for this chapter.

9.
—**I don't feel too good.**
—**What hurts?**
—**Nothing hurts, but I have a cough.**
—**Have you been to the doctor's?**
—**No, I haven't.**
—**You should go.**

Here we have a new verb "to hurt" **болеть**. If you have this funny feeling that the infinitve is the same as the verb "to be ill," ten browny points. It is the same infinitive, but it conjugates differently. Only the third person is used-**боли́т, боля́т**, and the question "What hurts" is rendered with the phrase "**Что у тебя (вас, него, ...) болит.**" This exercise has some good words to describe illnesses. Work on them. **насморк** and **кашель** are handy and take some practice, perhaps to learn. **температура** is easy, learn **высокая** if you don't know it yet.

This exercise also contrasts **был** and **сходить** for good measure.

10.
—**Did you go to the doctor's?**
—**Yes, I was at the doctor's.**
—**What did he say?**
—**He told me to lie in bed for three days.**

Here we have review of a whole bunch of handy-dandy constructions.

First, an unprefixed verb of motion to indicate a round trip-remember, review and learn-plus **к** and the dative to indicate "to whom" one went. Next, an equivalent phrase with **был** and the preposition **у** and the genitive to indicate "at whose place" (chez qui). Then we have a simple question, followed by the construction that we need to learn "**сказать, чтобы я лежал**" Review the idea of telling someone what to do and the construction **чтобы**+the subject+past tense.

Review the things that the doctor said to do-remember that "to take" medicine is "**принимать**". "**полоскать горло**" [to rinse the throat] means "to gargle." The other ones you should be able to figure out.

11.

—**My head really aches! Do you have anything for a headache?**
—**Yeah, I have some pills. Here.**
—**Thanks.**

Here we see the use of the construction "**у меня**" meaning "my." But the important construction to practice and learn here is "**от** + genitive of the ailment" to express "for +ailment" as in "for a headache" "for a toothache" "for a cough" and so on...

We also revisit the particles -**то** and -**нибудь**. In the first case the person wants to know if there is something (whatever it might be) for a headache. The rule of usually using -**нибудь** in a question works here. The -**то** is used in the answer because the person knows that there exists medicine, but not much else.

8.4▶

13.

—**Let's go for a stroll. The weather's great today.**
—**You don't think it's too cold today?**
—**No, warm is more like it.**
—**Let's go.**

Here we see again the use of **пойдём** as we did in ex. 6 of chapter 7, meaning "let's go" without **давайте**. Use it. Weather is introduced here just barely, but note the use of the comparative "**скорее**" meaning "more like it" or "sooner."
Learn the weather words - **прохладно**-cool 3. humid, dry.

14.

—**Do you happen to know what the temperature is today?**
—**It's hot today, 20 degrees [Celsius≈70 F.]**
—**How about tomorrow?**
—**Tomorrow it's going to be even hotter, 25.**

Typo in second dialogue.

More practice saying "Do you know...". Plus some practice getting tempatures and the right form of the word "degree" (nom., gen. sing, gen. plural). Furthermore, we practice the very useful comparatives "hotter" and "colder". Also some practice learning what is hot and what's not in degrees Celsius for Russians.

15.

—**Did you go to Tallinn?**
—**Yeah, last week we were in Tallinn.**
—**What was the weather like there?**
—**At first it was cold, and then it got warm.**
—**Was there any rain?**
—**Nope, it was dry.**
—**You were lucky. It often rains in Tallinn.**

The conversations are getting just a little longer. Here we once again encounter an unprefixed verb of motion used in the past to indicate a round trip **ездил куда**. This is contrasted, yet again, with **был** and the prepositional (**где**).

Note how we ask what the weather is/was like and the answer gives a bit of practice saying what was first and what was next. Rain is given in the genitive, and repeated in every instance. Notice again that there is a negative construction when asking for information (like the "**Вы не знаете, ...**" formula). Rain is wet so it is contrasted with **сухо**, not a major mental leap.

Note the very useful phrase for "You were lucky." This phrase is found almost exclusively in the past in Russian, so it ends up being used in contexts where in English we would say both "You were lucky" and "You are lucky." The construction is a dative of the agent and the word "повезло" [to say that one is habitually lucky we can use a present construction "тебе везёт"]

16.
—It is true that you lived in Arizona?
—Yup, I used to live in Arizona.
—What the weather there like in winter?
—In the winter it's cool in Arizona.
—How about in summer?
—Summers are hot in Arizona. [The summer is hot in Arizona]

Here we repeat the comparative **раньше**, learn it! We also practice the time expression "in the summer" and "in the winter". The phrase "in the winter" takes a adverbial "прохладно," whereas the last sentence uses the adjectival "жаркое" because "summer" is a noun here. Don't forget that Аляска and остров take на

8.5▶

17.
—It's so hot! Is the weather often hot here?
—No, as a rule, the weather's not so hot here.

First and foremost the completely new material is <u>on the tape!</u> The sixth "intonational construction" (IC-6) is introduced here. The intonation is typical of strongly "evaluative" sentences. The speaker wishes to add emphasis to the statement. Work on this intonation. The stressed syllable in the

This exercise practices the handy phrase **как правило**, and the use of **бывает** for expression of typical weather, and the use of the genitive after **не бывает**.

18.
—What a cold spring this year! Is the spring always so cold here?
—No, as a rule it's not so cold here in the spring.

More IC-6 practice. Here we contrast an adjectival construction "a cold spring" and an adverbial "so cold in the spring." Here we go over the seasons and the form for "in a season." Not hard, I hope.

20.
—How come John's not here?
—Because he got sick.
—I know why he got sick.
—Why?
—Because he was walking around without a hat on.
—And you think that that's why he got sick?
—Of course, I'm sure of it.

Points to be aware of: genitive of negation, **поэтому** as a word to indicate reason— "therefore"— and the short form adjective **уверен(а)**. **Поэтому** is introduced here because we are dealing with in this chapter various ways of expressing cause and effect. **Поэтому** indicates actual effect from actual cause, just like the word "therefore." [Therefore it's not surprising that **поэтому** is translated as "therefore.":—)]

Make sure you know all the reasons listed here for why someone would get sick.

21.
—How come you didn't go out for a walk?
—Because it started to rain.
—It started to rain and [therefore] that's why you didn't go out for a walk?
I would have gone.

This exercise illustrates again the use of **поэтому** (introducing a real cause from a real event) and introduces a conditional construction. This conditional is formed very simply in Russian—the particle **бы** and the past tense. The **бы**, like all particles, is unstressed and is pronounced together with the preceding word. It comes after the first stressed word in the sentence or right after the verb. [Since Russian doesn't have the myriad complex tenses of English, we rely on context to tell us whether this conditional phrase **я бы пошёл** means "I would have gone" or "I would go." I think you will agree with me that here we need "I would have gone." If we wanted to say "I would go" we would probably put in an adverb like **сейчас**]

8.6►

22.
—Are you going to go for a walk tomorrow?
—Yes, if my foot doesn't hurt.
—Is your foot still hurting.
—Yes, a little.

23.
—What are we going to do on Sunday?
—If the weather is good, we'll go to the countryside [out of town].
—And what if the weather is bad?
—We'll go to the exhibit.

24.
—Are you going to go to the exhibit.
—Absolutely [certainly I'll go], if I finish my work.
—And if you don't finish.
—Then I won't go.

Exercises 22, 23 and 24: In 22 we are recycling and reviewing our use of the verb of motion **пойти**, the imperfective future of **болеть** (and hence the infinitve constrasted with the present -**болит**), and the phrase **всё ещё** to stress "still." In 23 we have some time expression practice, and the expression **за́ город** (pronouned as one word, with the stress on **за**), and work with some possible leisure time activities. In 23 we have the verb **закончить**, in the future, and more future "to go" practice.

More importantly, however, is the introduction of **если**. Exercises 22, 23 and 24 all practice **если**. This is not a difficult word for us English speakers, "skoree" we overuse it. Nevertheless it is a real and useful word in Russian. The key thing to note in all these exercises is that after **если** we have a future! This is the expression of a "real condition." That is, when condition X is met, result Y will occur. In other words "Condition X will have to be met, then result Y will occur." You might be thinking "Why all the fuss, **если** is easy." The problem is that English speakers using Russian invariably use a present tense where they should use a future in the Russian. Pay attention to this. The rule is basically that if the main clause in Russian is in the future the **если** clause will be also. Since this is not the case in English, we need to watch out.

[hopefully you will see the cognitive connection here with **поэтому**, which we use when condition X has already been met, "therefore" result Y occurs]

2 5 .
—Olya came down with something again!
—She wouldn't have gotten sick if she had dressed more warmly.

2 6 .
—You wouldn't have gotten sick if you had dressed more warmly.
—You're probably right.
—I'm sure [that] I'm right.

2 7 .
—Write him a letter please.
—I would write it if my hand didn't hurt.

2 8 .
—Did you to Izmailovsky Park yesterday?
—No, we would have gone if there hadn't been a cold breeze.

2 9 .
—Did you go to Petrodvorets yesterday?
—No, we would have gone if it hadn't been cold.

Exercises 25-29 all deal with, most importantly, the use of **если бы**. This is the cause and effect structure most distant from real cause followed by real effect. It is used to express unreal conditions (ones that aren't, but if they were then something would happen). You can review this in PT-119. The construction itself is not so tough. We use **бы** as we did earlier we just put a **если** in in the conditional clause, and the **бы** remains in the effect clause to indicate that though it didn't occur it <u>would have</u>, had the condition been met.

The exercises keep to vocabulary that we have had, reviewing very conveniently things like the short form adjectives **прав** and **уверен**, the verbs **одеться, заниматься спортом** (to play sports), **задавать вопросы, обидеться** (to be offended—like I will be if you don't remember this verb), **выучить слова,** the vocabulary for parts of the body and place of rest and the weather that can spoil one's stay that these places. Make sure you know what all these things mean. Practice saying the sentences before coming to class.

[These constructions are introduced together and in this order because cause and effect are cognitive processes that have been shown in studies to be difficult to express. This is no joke. Human minds don't have much trouble recognizing things and naming them. My apologies to Chekhov drama lovers–this is a series of sentences built on the rifle in his play "Uncle Vanya."– We have no trouble saying "This is a play." "There is a rifle." "This is a play by Chekhov." Cause and effect is a little more difficult, "This is a play by Chekhov, therefore there is a rifle in it" Even more difficult for human minds is "If this is a play by Chekhov, then there is a rifle in it." Cognitively most difficult of all is the construction "If this were a play by Chekhov, there would be a rifle in it." Of course we can keep going: "If this were a play by Chekhov and there were a rifle in it, the rifle would go off" — Anybody who has seen "Howard's End" should remember the rifle and its effect in the movie—cleary taken straight from Chekhov. Since this sort of thinking is most difficult, it is not surprising that intermediate language students don't use them that often-we're struggling with describing things that <u>are,</u> not things that <u>might be</u>. Nevertheless, you need to begin to add these constructions to your arsenal of devices for expressing yourself as soon as possible—tomorrow, for instance :-)]

9.2▶

1.

—Have you done swimming for a long time?

—Yes, for a long time. I really love to swim.

—I would also like to do swimming, but I just don't have any free time.

3.

—What are you into? [What are you an avid fan of]

—I like to take photos.

—Do you spend a lot of time on photography?

—Yes, when I have time.

4.

—Is John interested in art?

—Yes, and he himself even draws.

—Does he draw well?

—Not bad.

—Did he start a long time ago?

—He's been drawing since childhood.

5.

—What do you do in your free time?

—I swim.

—Do you do aerobics?

—No, I'm not interested in aerobics at all.

Exercises 1-5 practice the use of nouns that will come in handy when talking about hobbies and interests. All the activities are pretty self-explanatory, and if your favorite hobby isn't here, find out how to say it and practice that one, too. All three of the exercises practice the use of verbs that take the instrumental case, so the question word will also be in the instrumental case. Be careful to use заниматься with nouns only. **For more detail on the use and meaning of these verbs you must read PT-126!**

Other things to note here are practice of the subjunctive particle **бы**, repetition of **сам**, the use of the imperfective after **начал** (ex. 4), and the right way to say "I don't have any free time".

9.3▶

6.

—Do you like to swim?

—Yes, I do.

—Does your brother swim, too?

—Yes, he swims better than any of us. He spends all his free time in the pool.

The exercise introduces the use of the verb **проводить** with **время**, to mean "to spend time." The good thing is that here all you have to know is the form **провóдит**. The exercise also gives us practice with the prepositional case learn which ones take **на** and which **в** (here 1,2,5,6 will take **на**), and remember the form for the adjectival prepositional.

8.

—What do you do in your free time?

—I'm interested in literature.

—What kind of literature interests you the most?

—Contemporary literature interests me most of all.

Now we have the tough contrast and use of the verb **интересовать** without **-ся**. Notice that this construction translates "interests you" instead of "you are interested in." The <u>agent</u> is in the accusative. The object of interest in in the nominative. This often causes problems for students, especially in contrast to **интересоваться**, so work on repeating the constructions for yourself.

"More" and "most of all" are also practiced here.

9.
—**What are you into?**
—**I collect stamps.**
—**Do you collect coins as well?**
—**No, coins don't interest me at all.**

For the collectors among us and you, and for those who know anybody that collects anything (that means all of us), this exercise needs to be practiced. No new grammar, per se, is introduced, but some good words are introduced. **значки** (2) are those little enamel pins that are so abundant in Russia.

9.4▶
11.
—**Where are you going?**
—**I'm going for a run.**
—**Do you often run.**
—**Yes, often. I'm used to running every day.**

Here we have some great practice with some useful words for activities (swimming, tennis, riding a bike, basketball and aerobics) —notice that the running and swimming are expressed with unprefixed multidirectional verbs of motion.

The new thing here is the word **привык, привыкла, привыкли**. It is followed by an imperfective infinitive and means "am/is/are <u>used to doing something</u>" [It might be nice to know that this is the past tense form of the perfective verb **привыкнуть**, and that the **ну** drops in the past, but for now all you have know is this form, it is by far the most common]

12.
—**Are you going for a run today?**
—**Yes, I want to go, but I'm a little afraid.**
—**Why**
—**Because I was sick for a whole month and got out of the habit of running.**

Here we have the opposite of **привыкнуть**. Depending on the context "To lose the knack for" "to become unaccustomed to," "to get out of practice" is rendered with **отвыкнуть**. Like **привыкнуть**, **отвыкнуть** is used almost only in the past, so just learn the form you need.

This exercise also practices a good word to express "a little" **немножко**. Otherwise the exercise is simply an excellent opportunity to practice the verbs **пойти**, **бояться (боюсь), болеть**, and to review the time expression **целый месяц**.

13.
—**How come you stopped? Don't you want to play any more?**
—**I want to, but I can't. I'm tired.**
—**What wrong?**
—**I haven't played in a long time and am out of practice.**

The big word to get your mouth around this time is **остановился, остановилась**. Learn it. It means "stopped." If you stop and think about it, the next phrase "any more" is sort of odd in English. The Russian construction **больше не** seems to make a little better sense — it might correspond to an English "no more".

Whatever the case, learn to use this construction. Also make sure you know the expression for "I am tired."

15.
—**Why aren't you doing aerobics anymore?**
—**I did aerobics for a whole year, and I got tired of doing aerobics.**
—**So what are you doing now?**
—**Now I'm into dancing.**

More practice with **больше не** and the introduction of **мне надоело** plus the imperfective infinitive. Then more practice with our favorite verbs of this chapter **заниматься** and **увлекаться**. Learn them, use them. Sound good.

16.
—**What were you into in childhood?**
—**For several years I collected stamps and amassed quite a collection.**
—**And do you collect them now?**
—**No, I got tired of collecting stamps.**

More practice with hobbies. Notice the use of the imperfective after **несколько лет**. The cues here are all given in the accusative, don't mess with the form, just learn all the other stuff that goes with it. [If you're interested you should note that the accusative of animate nouns is like the genitive in the masculine and plural {not in the feminine singular, of course} **кукла** is an animate noun, believe it or not.]

9.5▶

17-21
Ex. 17-21 practice the expression for "one of"—**один из** plus, of course, the genetive plural. There are three possible endings for nouns in the genitive plural (-ov, -ej or ∅). Adjectives (including substantivized nouns like **знакомый**) have only the ending -их in the genitive plural.

Ex. 17 only asks you to practice the gen. pl. of **знакомый**. Ex. 18 asks you to practice the gen. pl. of **они**, but also to make the **один** agree with the person, i.e. **одна из них моя сестра**. Ex. 19 finally asks you to form the gen. pl. of a number of nouns (the correct forms are: баскетболистов, преподавателей, теннисисток, солисток, студентов). Make sure you can do this before class. Ex. 20 and 21 work on the expression "one of my friends" (один из моих друзей, одна из моих подруг, один из моих знакомимых) Make sure you can do these correctly.

Otherwise these exercises review and "recycle" old material — ex. 17 is a variation on ex. 33 p.17. Ex. 18 reviews some verbs of motion and playing. 19 goes over clothes and colors. Exercise 20 is more practice with verbs of motion and activities. Exercise 21 is the same.

17.
—**Do have any friends who collect stamps.**
—**Yes, one of my acquaintances is a stamp collector.**
—**Can you introduce me to him?**
—**Sure I can.**

18.
—**Who's that running?**
—**One of them is my brother.**
—**And the other?**
—**I don't know who that is.**

19.
—Who's that over there
—Who? The girl in the blue bathing suit?
—Yes.
—That's one of our students.
—Do you know her.
—Yes, we swim together.

20.
—Did you run today?
—Yes, as always.
—Did you run alone?
—No, I ran with one of my friends.

21.
—Why weren't you at the pool?
—When I was on my way to the pool, I met a friend.
—So?
—And he suggested we go to a game.

9.6▶

22-24
Ex. 22-24 cover the expressions associated with playing instruments and games.
Refer to yesterday's homework for explanations if you need to. Note the verb **уметь** in 24 to mean "to know how to do something."

22.
—What that's music?
—That's my neighbor playing.
—Is he a musician?
—No, he just does it for fun [he's an amateur], but he plays the guitar very well.

23.
—Do you like music?
—Yes, very much.
—Do you play any instrument?
—Yes, I play the guitar. How about you?
—I don't play anything, but I like to listen to music.

24.
—Do you know how to play chess?
—No, I don't know how. Do you know how?
—A little. At one time I played well.

26, 28-30
Ex. 26 and 28-30 are good practice for talking about activities that we don't take part in but do enjoy watching. Make sure you know and can say all the kinds of competitions that are mentioned in ex. 26. Ex. 28 practices the expression for to win; 29 illustrates the expression for "to lose". Both go over the way to express the score. 30 gives the means to say that we were cheering for our friend or relation.

26.
—Today there's going to be an interesting sports program.
—Oh, yeah? What kind?

—A soccer game.
—At what time?
—At seven thirty. Let's watch it.
—Let's.

9.7▶

   28.
—Why weren't you at the game yesterday?
—Unfortunately, I couldn't go. Did you go?
—Of course I went.
—And who won?
—Our team won.
—What was the score.
—The score was 3 to 2.

   29.
—How come you're so down?
—There was a soccer game; I was rooting for our university team.
—Our team lost?
—I'll say [{"Lost"} is not the word]! The score was 1 to five.

   30.
—Where are you coming from?
—I'm [coming] the stadium.
—Did you play?
—No, I didn't.
—What were you doing there?
—I was watching soccer. I was rooting for my friend.

Exercises 1-9 introduce only a few new "grammatical" points:

Ex. 4 illustrates the use of the genitive of a direct object after a negated verb. If you use the genitive after a negated verb you'll be okay. You have to use it if the object is a pronoun. In 5 we have the construction "both ... and" as well as "neither ... nor...." It is a simpler construction in Russian "и...и" and "ни...ни". Otherwise, we have the introduction of some new vocabulary and practice with old vocabulary and constructions.

10.2▶

1.

—Where were you this summer?

—We went to the coast.

—Was it fun? [Are you satisfied?]

—Yes, it was wonderful.

Here we practice places, all in the accusative because of the verbs of motion practiced, and times when things happened. Go through the cues and make sure you know what to do with each of the times and the places. Don't forget that **концерт** takes **на**. Review the nouns that take **на** on p. 378 of the main text.

We also learn some words to describe a positive impression. **чудесно, замечательно, великолепно, отлично, прекрасно** basically they all mean "very good"—you need to know the words, and if you are a real dictionary fiend you can look these words up in various dictionaries and see if the dictionaries agree 100% with each other. Some English equivalents are: marvelous, wonderful, great, beautiful.

2.

—Do you happen to know where John went?

—He was at Lake Baikal

—What did he think [What were his impressions]

—He's happy.   He's planning to go again.

Here are some more places. These are little harder. Practice saying "**на Соловецких островах**" [The plural of **остров** (island) is **острова́**. This is good to know.] You should be comfortable with **впечатления** (lesson 7, ex. 12) and **собираться**.

3.

—Where did Alan go?

—He didn't go anywhere.

—Why?

—I don't know, I haven't talked to him about that yet.

Here the major point is practice with negation and the use of the particle **ни**. We also repeat the construction **мы с ним**.

4.

—Where did you take your holiday.[Where did you vacation.]

—In Yalta.

—Did you like it there?

—Very much.   Especially the sea.

—The sea?

—Yes, I've never seen such a blue sea.

This introduces the use of the genitive for direct objects of negated verbs. Watch out for the genitive plurals in 2,4,5 and 7,(**не видел таких белых ночей**.) There is also good practice with the prepositional plural in 2,4,5 and 7.

5.

—Sasha has still not been to either England or America.

—I have been to England and America, but I still haven't been in either Japan or Cuba.

—I have been to Japan and Cuba, but I still haven't been in either ...

This can be a round-game type exercise where each person needs to remember the places mentioned by the previous person, say that they haven't been to either of those places and then say that they <u>have</u> been to two other places. Remember that "in the Crimea" is в Крымý.

10.3▶

6.

—I heard [They told me], that you were in Egypt.

—Yes, last week.

—How did you like it?

—It's wonderful there. But the weather surprised me.

—Why?

—It was cold.

Here we work on some places, some time expressions (please review them), and the new word удивить in the construction меня удивила погода.

7.

—What did you like most on the trip?

—Everything was great, but the greatest thing was the lake.

This exercise might cause some problems because of the construction ...самое замечательное—это озеро. The words самое замечательное in this sentence mean "The most wonderful *thing*. Thus, structurally the meaning of the whole utterance might be conveyed, "the most wonderful *thing*—this is the lake" That isn't good English, and that's why we don't accept structural translations. We might see it better if we take number 2. самое замечательное—это горы.

8.

—What did Sasha like there?

—He didn't like anything.

—Really?

—Yes, he was in a bad mood.

Here we have a simple universal reason not to do something, being in a bad mood. Notice that the Russian construction is structurally not "in" but "has." We also work on the complete negation of things "didn't like anything." Make sure you can put the cues in dative. Try putting 4 and 10 in the мы с ... type construction.

9.

—Did you like your trip?

—No, not at all.

—Why?

—It was boring there.

—Boring?

—Yes, the people weren't very interesting.

Here are some reasons not to like something, besides just being in bad mood. Work on the words so that you can make a good impression in class.

11.

—**Where did you vacation?**
—**We went to the Solovetskie islands.**
—**Really? How did you get there?**
—**We went by train to Archangelsk.**
—**A then?**
—**And from Archangelsk we flew by plane.**

Here the central practice point is the verb **добраться**. If you can, learn to conjugate it: доберусь, доберёшься, доберутся, добрался, добралáсь, добрáлись. If you can't, at least learn the form here. Also pay attention to the two constructions for expressing mode of transportation: the instrumental case without a preposition, and **на** plus the prepositional case.

Briefly about the places mentioned: Linda writes about Solovetskie islands in her diary—Archangel is the nearest big city, Krasnodar is a city near, but not on, the Black Sea. Irkutsk is a large Siberian city 45 miles from lake Baikal, the deepest lake in the world. Ясная поляна is Lev Tolstoy's estate, Tula is a city famous for samovars (the Russian metal urn used to boil water for tea). Tula is not far from Moscow. Михайловское was one of the estates in western Russia of the poet Alexander Pushkin. Pskov is the nearest big city, and a historically important Russian city. Юрмола is a resort city near the Baltic city of Riga in Latvia. Кижи is an open air park/museum of old Russian wooden architecture. Феропонтов монастырь is a famous northern monastery near the beautiful northern city of Vologda.

12.

—**Where do you want to go in the summer?**
—**I want to go to Lake Seliger.**
—**Where's that?**
—**It's in the central part of Russia.**
—**How are you going to get there?**
—**We're going to go by car.**

Here we have some more practice with the prepostional of places. Almost all the cues have something tricky about them, so if you're not sure about the preposition or form needed to answer the cues, see p. 378.

13.

—**I know that you wanted to go to Petersburg. Shall we go together?**
—**I've already been.**
—**Really, when?**
—**Last week.**

Here we use the verb **съездить** in the past to indicate one round trip. The tricky thing here is that somewhere someone told us that prefixes added to multidirectional verbs of motion produce imperfective verbs [of course we have no problem with the idea that the concept of multidirectional and unidirectional exists only in unprefixed verbs of motion, and that unprefixed verbs of motion are <u>all,</u> without exception, no lie, <u>all</u> imperfective]. When the prefix **c-** adds the meaning "a single round trip" it is added to multidirectional verbs and is perfective.

14.

—Is this your first time in Washington?
—Yes, the first time.
—Do you like Washington?
—Yes, it is very pretty.
—Have you already been to the National Gallery?
—Yes, we've already been there. It is wonderful.

Here the important thing to notice is the use of the phrase **ты первы раз** meaning "your first time." Otherwise the exercise is good practice with previously introduced material.

10.5▶

15.

—Do you want to go to the National Gallery?
—Yes, but I'm free only until 12.
—Let's go. It's not far from here.
—Will we make it there and back by 12?
—Yes, of course we'll make it.

The only new point here is one of conversational syntax. Ellipsis, the omission of a word not necessary for the comprehension of a sentence, is a common feature of spoken Russian. Here we find it in **Мы успеем туда и обратно до двенадцати**? We might expect a perfective infinitive after **успеем**, such as **сходить**, but the context makes it clear, and the verb is left out. The other new phrase is **вы не хотите...** as a suggestion formula. Note the use of the **не**. It is similar to the **не** in **Вы не знаете**.

The rest of this dialogue is practice with material that we have had earlier.

16.

—Have you already been to Petrodvorets?
—Yes, we went there yesterday.
—Who did you go with?
—We went with Boris.

More practice here with the use of the verb **съездить** to mean one round trip [attached to verbs of motion the prefix **с-** has another meaning as well,. It adds the meaning "descent" when context indicates (usually with the preposition **с** and the genitive. With this meaning it acts like other prefixes when added to the unprefixed verbs of motion — when added to multidirectional it produces an imperfective with a perfective pair made from the unidirectional with the same prefix. Thus **Он сошёл с автобуса**. "He got off of the bus." or, for that matter **Они сходят с ума**, "They are going off their rockers." "They going out of their minds." The prefix **с-** when with the particle **-ся** has yet another meaning — "to gather, come together." This is just a sample of some of the wonderful things still to learn in Russian, and here only for information and curiosity's sake.]

The exercise also provides some practice with the instrumental, and the use of the multidirectional unprefixed verb in the past tense to indicate round trip (yes, in this context a basic synonym for **съездить** and, for that matter, **был**).

When you are saying number 3, remember that **с Ирой** will be pronounced **сЫрой** because the «**с**» is hard.

17.

—The park is so beautiful! Shall we walk some more?
—Ok, only just a little.
—Let's walk a little, and then go to the movies.
—Great! [we've agreed!]

INTONATION! The problem with this intonation is that is carries emotional expressiveness that requires you to "act" to get the right sound in these exercises. However, you need to do it. Remember that the first person plural form can mean "Let's". The prefix **по-** is reviewed here with the meaning "to start off for" or really just to make the verb perfective since the context, consecutive actions, requires it. This is in anticipation of introducing **по-** with another meaning in ex. 18.

Learn **Договорились** as a response of agreement when wrapping up a conversation and confirming plans.

18.

—Have you already seen the old part of the city?
—Yes, in drove around a little there in the evening.
—Too bad that it was just a little. It is so pretty.
—Yes, I agree, but we had very little time.

Here we have the use of the prefix **по-** with the meaning "for a little while." In this instance the addition of **по-** to the multidirectional, as with the prefix **с-**, produces a perfective verb. Thus **походим немного** means "we <u>will</u> walk around a little." In the past the **по-** indicates emphasis on the idea that the action was "for a little while." Here, and often an adverb is added to underscore this idea, but this is not necessary.

10.6▶

19.

—Why are you so late?
—On the way we stopped at the exhibit.
—So?
—We wanted to just walk around a bit, but it was so interesting that we spent a full two hours walking through the exhibit.

Here the major point is the introduction of the prefix **про-** which can be added to multidirectional verbs of motion for perfective temporal (as opposed to spatial) meaning, **про-**. If you look back to page 62 you will see exercises 38b, and 39, that illustrate the use of the prefix **про-** with purely spatial meaning "to drive, walk, fly <u>by</u> something." (Recall that we had in Lesson 2 verbs of motion with the prefixes **при-, у-, вы-, под-, про-**. We have also had **по-** and **за-**). Notice that in the translation the English uses the verb "spent" for the idea of the time and "walking through the exhibit" to convey the meaning of walking. The "exhibit" is added in the English translation to make it sound more natural.

21.

—Do you like this [thing]?
—Very much. Where did you get it from?
—My brother brought if for me from Spain.
—He was in Spain?
—Yes, he returned from there not long ago.

Here we practice the past tense of the prefixed transitive verb of motion **привезти**, and the past of the verb **вернуться** "to return."Then more practice with places. 1, and 5 take **на** and **с**.

22.

—Where did you get such a pretty tee-shirt?
—I brought it from Egypt.
—You were in Egypt?
—Yes, this summer.

The construction **откуда у тебя (у него, у неё ...)** plus a thing in the nominative is structurally quite different from the English equivilent construction "Where did you get..." For this reason it can be difficult to remember and use. Practice it. Make it yours. More practice with **привезти** in the past. Then more practice with Egypt with its fleeting "e" and other places and times.

10.7▶

24.

—Have you been on that bank [of the lake]?
—Yes, I have.
—The view of the lake is best from there, isn't it?
—Yes, I have never seen such beauty.

The form **на берегу** should not be strange to you. Recall that there is a group of nouns that take stressed **у́** in the prepositional (see p. 378 in the text if you don't recall). Other than the vocabulary, we also review here the use of the genitive for the direct object of a negated verb. Notice that **вид на** takes the accusative so, for instance, 2 will be

Правда, оттуда самый красивый вид на набережную.

Набережная meanis "embankment" and is used to described the embankments along the Neva in St. Petersburg and the buildings that line them. In number 3 you should be able to recognize the root **смотр+** in **смотровая площадка** and see why it means "viewing platform."

25.

-Shall we go over there?
—What can you see from over there?
—The prettiest cathedral is visible from there.

Here we're practicing only the short form adj. **видно**. It agrees in gender and number with that which is seen. It doesn't decline, and if the subject is something like **что** or **всё** the form **видно** is used.

26.

—Have you climbed that mountain?
—Not yet.
—You really must. The whole coast is visible from there.
—Yes, everyone says that everything is visible from there.

Here the word to learn is **обязательно**. Also note that the question **вы поднимались...** is in the imperfective because the act of climbing has been negated by the fact that the person has no descended. Recall our use of prefixed multidirectional verbs of motion that have this sort of meaning in the past, see the model for ex. 14, p. 194. Otherwise there's not too much to do but make sure you know how to manipulate the cues.

27.

a. Having left Washington, we remember this.
—**When did you remember about this?**
—**We remembered when we had left Washington.**
b. Leaving (While leaving) Washington, we bought souvenirs
—**When did you buy the souvenirs?**
—**We bought souvenirs when we were leaving Washington.**

Ex. 27 works on recognition of verbal adverbs (many English-Russian dictionaries refer to this form as "gerunds"). The model sentences reflect the meaning of these adverbials. The ones in 27a are called past or perfective gerunds, the ones in 27b are present gerunds. They show either sequence or simultaneous action. Except in a few standard phrases like "honestly speaking" **честно говоря** they are not often used in spoken Russian. Here you are only asked to understand what they mean (do that by recognizing the underlying verb) and rephrasing the situation into spoken form. Imperfective verbal adverbs indicate simultaneous actions ("doing something" person X did, does or will do something else). They are recognizable by the letter -**я** added to the stem of the verb. Perfective verbal adverbs indicate consecutive action ("having done something"person X did, does or will do something else). They are recognizable by the letter -**в** added to the stem of the verb. If the verb is reflexive the ending is -**вшись**. You need to be able to recognize these forms. For more practice look at the first commentary to the first reading selection on pg. 37.

Письменные задания

Урок 1: Письменные задания

1.1

stem	представля́й+ся	предста́ви+ся	знако́ми+ся	нра́ви+ся
infinitive	представля́ться	предста́виться	знако́миться	нра́виться
non-past				
я	представля́юсь	предста́влюсь	знако́млюсь	нра́влюсь
ты	представля́ешься	предста́вишься	знако́мишься	нра́вишься
он, она́, оно́	представля́ется	предста́вится	знако́мится	нра́вится
мы	представля́емся	предста́вимся	знако́мимся	нра́вимся
вы	представля́етесь	предста́витесь	знако́митесь	нра́витесь
они́	представля́ются	предста́вятся	знако́мятся	нра́вятся
past				
он	представля́лся	предста́вился	знако́мился	нра́вился
она́	представля́лась	предста́вилась	знако́милась	нра́вилась
они́	представля́лись	предста́вились	знако́мились	нра́вились

1.4

Моего отца зовут Джефф. Его зовут Джефф.
Его брата зовут Том. Его зовут Том.
Его сестру зовут Анна. Её зовут Анна.
Мою сестру зовут Нина. Её зовут Нина.
Её отца зовут Иван. Его зовут Иван.
Моего друга зовут Саша. Его зовут Саша.
Мою соседку зовут Наташа. Её зовут Наташа.
Меня зовут Линда. (Её зовут Линда)

1.5

nom.	acc.	gen.
знакомый	знакомого	знакомого
учёный	учёного	учёного
dat.	prep.	inst.
знакомому	ознакомом	знакомым
учёному	об учёном	учёным

1.6

2. Кто эта женщина?
   Это Ольга Петровна. Она моя знакомая.
   А кто она?
   Она преподавательница.
5. Кто этот человек?
   Это Николай Борисович. Он мой знакомый.
   А кто он?
   Он преподаватель.

1.7

2. Да, он поля́к.
7. Да, они итальянцы
15. Да, он грек (она гречанка)

1.9

3. Да, французский — мой родной язык.

4. Да, арабский — её родной язык.

5. Да, немецкий — его родной язык.

1.10

3. Он француз, но он очень хорошо знает финский язык и говорит по-фински свободно, без акцента.

4. Она итальянка, но она очень хорошо знает английский язык и говорит по-английски свободно, без акцента.

5. Мы русские, но мы очень хорошо знаем французский язык и говорим по-французски свободно, без акцента.

3б. Он француз и плохо знает финский язык. Он говорит по-фински с трудом, с акцентом.

4б. Она итальянка и плохо знает английский язык. Она говорит по-английски с трудом с акцентом.

5б. Мы русские и плохо знаем французский язык. Мы говорим по-французски с трудом, с акцентом.

1.14

2. Шеррелл учится в Пенсильванском университете. Она занимается историей.

3. Наташа учится в Московском университете. Она занимается биологией.

6. Ира учится в энергетическом институте. Она занимается кибернетикой.

1.16

1. Она специалист по экологии моря.

3. Он специалист по истории искусства.

4. Он специалист по современной американской литературе.

5. Я специалист по психологии.

1.17.а

1. Моя подруга работает секретарём в госдепартаменте.
2. Кристина работает официанткой в китайском ресторане.
3. Инна работает переводчиком в информационном бюро.
4. Мой брат работает редактором в городской газете.

1.20

работы, работник, работают, безработный

1.24
единственное число

им	дочь	сестра́	мать
вин	дочь	сестру́	мать
род	до́чери	сестры́	ма́тери
дат	до́чери	сестре́	ма́тери
пред	о до́чери	о сестре́	о ма́тери
твор.	до́черью	сестро́й	ма́терью

множественное число

им	до́чери	сёстры	матери
вин	дочере́й	сестёр	матере́й
род	дочере́й	сестёр	матере́й
дат	дочеря́м	сёстрам	матеря́м
пред	о дочеря́х	о сёстрах	о матеря́х
твор.	дочерьми́	сёстрами	матеря́ми

1.25
1. Нет, у меня нет квартиры, но у меня есть комната.
2. Нет, у меня нет сестры, но у меня есть брат.
3. Нет, у меня нет дочери, но у меня есть сын.
4. Нет, у меня нет бабушки, но у меня есть дедушка.

1.26
1. Нет, у меня нет красной ручки. У меня только чёрная ручка. 4. Нет, у меня нет сегодняшней газеты. У меня только вчерашняя газета. 8. Нет, у меня нет маленького стола. У меня только большой стол.

1.30
1. смешно. 2. милы 3. скучно 4. ясно 5. грустно 6. интересная 7. лёгкое

1.32
моя семья, 2. моей семьи 3. мою семью 4. моей семье 5. моей семьёй 6. моей семье

1.33
а. Виктор женат на Наташе, Джон женат на Линде, Иван женат на Лене, Стив женат на Кристине
Наташа замужем за Виктором. Линда замужем за Джоном. Лена замужем за Иваном. Кристина замужем за Стивом.
б. Света не замужем. Сергей не женат, Нил не женат, Шеррел не замужем, Роман не женат.

1.34

Я хочу познакомить вас с моей семьёй. Это фотография моей семьи. Это моя мать. Её зовут Анна Николаевна. Она журналист. Она раньше работала за границей, в Америке, а сейчас она работает в Москве в большом информационном агенстве. Это мой отец, Олег Иванович. Он директор новой фирмы. Он много работает. И это мой брат. Он ещё учится и хочеть стать адвокатом. Это наша сестра Лена. Она замужем. Она и муж, Иван, живут в Санкт Петербурге. Она учится в Санкт Петербургском университете, на экономическом факультете. У Ивана своя фирма, он директор строительной компании.

1.35

3. 1. Он спросил, где я живу (где он/а живёт). 2. Она спросила, откуда он приехал. 3. Олег спросил меня, работаю ли я. 4. Таня спросила, придёт ли Саша вечером. 5. Сосед спросил ездил ли я вчера к родителям. 6. Они спросили меня, работаю ли я в банке.

1.39

б. 1. место, 2. место, место 3. поместились, 4. помещались

1.40

читатель читает, преподаватель преподаёт, издатель издаёт, исследователь исследует

продавет продаёт, программист программирует, консультант консультирует, переводчик переводит

1.42

Моя подруга Кристина родилась в Америке, но её мать из Испании и её отец из Франции. Её мать приехала в Америку когда ей было пять лет и она говорит по-английски свободно. Её отец тоже говорит без акцента. Но они не забыли свои родные языки. Дома у Кристины говорят по-французски, по-испански и по-английски. Кристина знает английский, испанский и французский. Недавно она начала заниматься русским языком. Но она плохо говорит по-русски. Она уже была за границей—во Франции и в Испании. Её дядя живёт в Испании. Он адвокат (юрист). Её бабушка живёт в Испании. Она больше не работает. У неё свой дом. Кристина ещё не была в России, но она будет учиться там осенью.

stem	встреча́й+ся	встре́ти+ся	догова́ривай+ся	договори́+ся	находи́й+ся
infinitive	встреча́ться	встре́титься	догова́риваться	договори́ться	находи́ться
non-past					
я	встреча́юсь	встре́чусь	догова́риваюсь	договорю́сь	нахожу́сь
ты	встреча́ешься	встре́тишься	догова́риваешься	договори́шься	нахо́дишься
он, она́, оно́	встреча́ется	встре́тится	догова́ривается	договори́тся	нахо́дится
мы	встреча́емся	встре́тимся	догова́риваемся	договори́мся	нахо́димся
вы	встреча́етесь	встре́титесь	догова́риваетесь	договори́тесь	нахо́дитесь
они́	встреча́ются	встре́тятся	догова́риваются	договоря́тся	нахо́дятся
past					
он	встреча́лся	встре́тился	догова́ривался	договори́лся	находи́лся
она́	встреча́лась	встре́тилась	догова́ривалась	договори́лась	находи́лась
они́	встреча́лись	встре́тились	догова́ривались	договори́лись	находи́лись

2.2c

1.близко ближайшей
2. порядок
3. близкий
4. рядом
5. Ближнем востоке
6. напротив
7. близнецы
8. недалеко
9. дальнему
10. противоречий

2.3

а1. нет зрителей 2. зрителей 3. со зрителями 4. о зрителях
б. 1. прохожий   2. прохожего   3. прохожему   4. прохожего 5. с прохожим, о прохожем
с. 1. рынок 2. рынок   3. на рынке 4. рынком   5. рынка   6. к рынку

2.4c

1. выход   2. у входа   3. вышла замуж   4. прохожего

2.8

а. Я работаю в международном банке. Банк находится недалеко от моего дома. Это очень красивый старый район. Старая почта находится рядом с большим новым банком. Напротив банка маленький ресторан. Я обычно там обедаю.

б. Стив живёт в маленькой квартире в большом новом доме. Дом находится далеко от центра города, но есть станция метро рядом с домом. Между станцией метро и домом находится маленький парк. Справа от дома - большой магазин. Стиву очень нравится этот район.

2.9
1. Джон часто ездит (ходит) на консультацию к преподавателю.
4. Мы часто ездим (ходим) на стадион к тренеру.
6. Я часто езжу зá город к родителям.

2.10
1. Этот автобус идёт в Филадельфию.
3. Зрители бегут к входу в цирк.
5. Этот самолёт летит из Копенгагена.

2.11
1. идёшь, иду, ходишь
2. бегу, бежишь, бегу
3. едешь, еду, ездишь, езжу

2.13
1. Когда я шла в университет, ко мне подошёл ....
4. Когда она летела в Москву, она познакомилась...
6. Когда он ехал в поезде из Петербурга в Москву, он познакомился ...

2.16
1. на машине
2. на такси
3. два часа
4. на самолёте

2.19
1. едет
2. ездит
3. идут
4. ходят
5. бегут
6. бегают
7. езжу, еду

2.20
1. летать, ездит, летит
2. плавает, плывёт
3. езжу, еду
4. ездить, еду

2.23
1. Они ездили на эксурсию в Третьяковскую галерию.
3. Она ездила к родителям.
5. Они ездили в Польшу, в Варшаву.
7. Он летал в Крым, на море.

2.25
1. ходили, шли
3. ехал
6. ездила
8. ходил, шёл

2.26c

1. водительские права, водит
2. на подносе
3. вывозить
4. международных отношений
5. переводчик, экскурсоводом
6. Унесённые ветром

2.28

1. Самолёт летит на север, везёт почту.
3. носят словари
6. везёт нефть
8. несут грибы и ягоды.

2.29

1. нёс
2. во́зит
3. ношу́
4. во́дит
5. но́сит
6. вози́ла
7. несёт

2.30

stem	предлага́й	предложи́+	приглаша́й+	пригласи́+
infinitive	предлага́ть	предложи́ть	приглаша́ть	пригласи́
non-past				
я	предлага́ю	предложу́	приглаша́ю	приглашу́
ты	предлага́ешь	предло́жишь	приглаша́ешь	пригласи́шь
он,она́, оно́	предлага́ет	предло́жит	приглаша́ет	пригласи́т
мы	предлага́ем	предло́жим	приглаша́ем	пригласи́м
вы	предлага́ете	предло́жите	приглаша́ете	пригласи́те
они́	предлага́ют	предло́жат	приглаша́ют	пригласи́т
past				
он	предлага́л	предложи́л	приглаша́л	пригласи́л
она́	предлага́ла	предложи́ла	приглаша́ла	пригласи́ла
они́	предлага́ли	предложи́ли	приглаша́ли	пригласи́ли

2.34

поехать, пойду, поедем, пойдём, пойдём

2.35

1.Наташа предлагает мне пойти в джаз клуб.
3.Борис предлагает Шеррелл пойти в кино.
6.Андрей предлагает нам пойти на день рождения.

2.37

а.
1. Анна пришла на урок из библиотеки.
3. Он приедет домой с работы в пять часов.
5. Они пришли в общежитие из компьютерного центра

б.
1. ушли из аудитории
3. ушли из зрительного зала
5. ушла из посольства

2.38
1. приехал, уезжают (уедут)
2. приезжали, уехали
3. приходит, уходит
4. приезжают, уезжают
5. пришли, ушли

2.39
1. я пришёл в кинотеатр за полчаса до начала фильма.
3. Я уехал из университета за пять дней до конца семестра.
6. Я ушёл из консерватории за двенадцать минут до конца концерта.

2.41
1. въезжает
2. выходит
3. вбега́ет
7. выходя́т

2.42
1. вошёл
2. вышла
3. выезжает
4. вошли
5. вошла
6. вышла

2.44
1. отошёл от стола
2. подошёл к доске
3. подходит к платформе
4. отъехало от вокзала
5. отходят от остановки
6. отошла от прохожего
7. отошёл от меня

2.45
поехать, вышли, поехали, приехали, ушёл, пошли, подошёл, вошли, отошёл, ехали, приехали, вышли, пошли, поехали.

2.46.b
1. много, Многие   2. много, Многие
3. много, Многие   4. много, Многие

2.47.b

1. Несколько, некоторые
2. несколько, некоторые
3. несколько, некоторые
4. несколько, некоторые
5. несколько, некоторые

2.48

1. бежало, бежали
2. шло, шли
3. ехало, ехали
4. стояло, ждали

2.49

На уроке русского языка много студентов. Некоторые из них иностранцы. Многие из нас и работают и учатся. Многие из нас снимают квартиры или живут с родителями.

2.50

1. Линда спросила когда начало спектакля.
2. Саша спросил(а) Линду, когда они встретятся.
3. Линда спросила, где находится новый цирк
4. Линда спросила прохожего, как доехать до Цветного бульвара.
5. Саша спросила Линду, не хочет ли она пойти в цирк.
6. Линда спросила, Старый ли это цирк.
7. Подружки спросили Машу, пойдёт ли она с ними в лес за грибами.
8. Медведь спросил Машеньку, не умеет ли она кашу варить.

2.52. a

-Привет Наташа!
-Привет Джон!
-Куда ты спешишь?
-Я иду на урок английского языка, а ты?
-Я иду в столовую.
-Давай встретимся после урока.
-Договорились.
-Я буду тебя ждать у входа в библиотеку.
-Пока.

б. (в метро)
-Привет Боб!
-Привет Сергей!
-Откуда ты идёшь?
-Я иду из центра. Я работаю на бирже в центре. А ты откуда идёшь?
-Я был у приятеля.

c.

Вчера вечером звонила Света и пригласила меня пойти в кино. Мы согласились встретиться за десять минут до начала у входа в кино. Кинотеатр находится недалеко от моего дома, и я решил идти пешком. Я вышел из дома за полчаса до начала фильма. Я прошёл через парк, перешёл улицу и подошёл к кинотеатру. Я пришёл вовремя на место встречи. Света уже меня ждала. Мы купили билеты, вошли в зал. После фильма мы пошли вместе в ресторан. Я пришёл домой очень поздно.

2.55

stem	собирáй+ся	собра+ся
infinitive	собирáться	собрáться
non-past		
я	собирáюсь	соберýсь
ты	собирáешься	соберёшься
он,онá, онó	собирáется	соберётся
мы	собирáемся	соберёмся
вы	собирáетесь	соберётесь
они́	собирáются	соберýтся
past		
он	собирáлся	собрáлся
онá	собирáлась	собралáсь
они́	собирáлись	собрали́сь

<u>Урок 3: Письменные задания</u>

3.3c
1. во́время
2. современная
3. современики
4. временно
5. времени
6. во время

3.5c
1. рано
2. опаздать
3. поздно
4. раньше
5. раннюю
6. позднюю

3.7
1. Они приехали вчера вечером в семь часов
2. Она уехала сегодня днём в два часа.
3. Он прилетает завтра ночью в три часа.
4. Он уезжает завтра вечером в девять часов.
5. Он сказал мне об этом вчера утром в десять часов.

3.8.a
1. ... а вчера он лёг спать в двадцать минут двенадцатого.
2. ... а вчера она встала в половине девятого.
3. ... а вчера мы обедали в два часа.
4. ... а вчера мы ужинали в половине восьмого.

b
1. ... а сегодня я лягу спать в десять часов.
2. ... а завтра он встанет в половине седьмого.
3. ... а сегодня мы пообедаем без четверти час.
4. ... а сегодня лягут спать в восемь часов.

3.9.a
1. Да, с двенадцати часов.
2. Да, с девяти часов.
3. Да, с двух часов.
4. Да, с часа.
5. Да, с трёх

b
1. Да, до шести часов.
2. Да, до пяти часов.
3. Да, до восьми часов.
4. Да, до семи часов.

3.12

1. Они приедут на этой неделе, в среду.
2. Экзамен будет на следующей неделе, в пятницу.
3. Мы его купили на прошлой неделе, в понедельник.
4. Экзамен будет на будущей неделе, в четверг.

3.13

1. Она родилась зимой, в феврале.
3. Они начинаются летом, в июне.
6. Мы поедем в Москву летом, в августе.
9. День независимости в Америке летом, в июле.
12. Она родилась осенью, в октябре.

3.14

1. Завтра мне некогда, у меня совсем не будет свободного времени.
3. Во вторник мне некогда, у меня совсем не будет свободного времени.

3.15

1. С детства
2. с раннего утра
5. с прошлого года
7. со вторника

3.16

1. со школы
3. со следующей недели
5. с декабря прошлого года.

3.17

1.Она поедет через месяц
4. Она начнётся через пятнадцать минут
7. Я закончу университет через год.

3.18

3. Мы можем приехать на три дня.
4. Они уезжают на месяц.

3.19

4. Наши знакомые собираются в Африку. Они поедут на три недели. Они там будут жить три недели. Они вернутся через три недели.

3.20

2. Они приехали за несколько дней до начала конференции.
5. Я пришёл за две минуты до начала лекции.

3.21

3. Когда твоя сестра родилась?
5. Когда вы обычно встаёте?
8. Когда механик начинает работать? (there are other right questions to this one)

3.23
1. писал
2. построили
3. писал
4. выучил
5. проводит
6. перевёл
7. читали
8. печатал
9. написал

3.24a
.(possible answers—others are also possible)
1. Потому, что я готовил(а) обед.
2. Я готовил(а) обед
3. Да, я приготовил(а) обед.
4. Я готовил(а) обед
5. Да, я его приготовил(а).

3.24b
1. Я переводил(а) текст
2. Нет, я должен/должна перевести текст. или Нет, я ещё не перевёл/перевела текст.
3. Я переводил(а) текст.
4. Нет, я ещё не перевёл/перевела его.
5. Нет, не могу, я перевожу текст. Да, после того, как перведу текст.

3.26.c
1. начал
2. конечной
3. Начало
4. наконец
5. Сначала
6. начинаются, кончаются

3.27.c
1. успел
2. успехов
3. спешу
4. успешно

3.29
1. одеваться
2. приготовить
3. написать
4. собирать
5. составлять
6. прочитать
7. говорить
8. представиться
9. прощаться
10. спросить
11. отвечать

3.32

(other sentences are possible-use the conjunctions from ex. 31.)

1. В то время, как Ольга одевала детей, Дима накрывал на стол к завтраку.

2. Пока она ехала на работу, она читала повесть...

3.33.a

1. После того, как Саша купил билеты, он позвонил Линде и пригласил её в цирк.

2. После того, как Ольга посмотрела журналы, она их дала мне.

3. После того, как она прочитала статью, она начала составлять график.

4. После того, как она поставила будильник, она легла спать.

б.

1. До того, как Саша купил билтеы, он позвонил Линде и пригласил её в цирк.

2. До того, как Ольга посмотрела журналы, она их дала мне.

3. До того, как она прочитала статью, она начала составлять график.

4. До того, как она поставила будильник, она легла спать.

3.35

1. сам

2. самому (самой)

3. самим

4. сама

5. сами

6. самим

3.36.a

1. Линда свободна после ужина

2. Студенты свободны после занятий

3. Я свободна после работы

4. Они свободны после спектакля

5. Мы свободны после лекции

6. Борис свободен после обеда

б

1. Линда была свободна после ужина

2. Студенты были свободны после занятий

3. Я была свободна после работы

4. Они были свободны после спектакля

5. Мы были свободны после лекции

6. Борис был свободен после обеда

3.37.а

1. Кэти занята до пяти часов.
2. Том занят до одиннадцати часов.
3. Механик занят до четырёх часов.
4. Студенты заняты до двух часов.
5. Мы заняты до часа.
6. Я занят(а) до вечера.

б

1. Кэти будет занята до пяти часов.
2. Том будет занят до одиннадцати часов.
3. Механик будет занят до четырёх часов.
4. Студенты будут заняты до двух часов.
5. Мы будем заняты до часа.
6. Я буду занят(а) до вечера.

3.38

1. свободно
2. свободен
3.свободного
4. свобода
5.свободно

3.39

уже, ещё, ещё, ещё, уже, ещё

3.40

1. Нет, ещё не обедала.
2. Нет, ещё не брился.
3. Нет, ещё не искал.
5. Нет, ещё не мыл.
6. Нет, ещё не одевал.

3.41

1. Я читал, но не прочитал.
3. Я готовил его, но не приготовил.
4. Я искала но не нашла.

3.42.а

—Ты знаешь, скоро будет день рождения Олега?
—Когда?
—Десятого января
—А сегодня какое число?
—Сегодня седьмое.
—Значит, у него день рождения через три дня?
—Да, и он уже нас пригласил к себе.

б

—Вы не скажете когда этот магазин работает?
—С девяти утра до семи вечера.
—А в воскресенье он открыт?
—Нет, в воскресенье он закрыт.

3.46c

1.одевает, одевается
2. одежду
3. раздевайтесь
4. Одевайся
5. надевал

3.48

1. умывается, умывает
2. умывает
3. умываться

1. одеваться
2. одевает, одевается
3. одевать
4. оделся

1. бреется
2. брил
3. брить
4. (по)брился

1. причесаться
2. причёсывать
3. причесал
4. причёсывается

3.52

Стив учится в университете Айовы. Обычно он встаёт в семь часов. По понедельникам, средам и пятницам у него уроки с девяти до часа. Обычно он обедает с часа до двух. После обеда по вторникам и четвергам он работает механиком в гараже. Когда нет занятий в университете, он занимается в библиотеке или работает в компьютерном центре утром. Библиотека открывается в девять, и когда Стив приходит в университет до девяти он обычно идёт в компьютерный центр, который открыт круглосуточно. В субботу и воскресенье он часто ездит к девушке, которая живёт недалеко от университета. Два раза в год, зимой и весной, Стив ездит к родителям в Калифорнию.

4.1

stem	грусти+ (ст-щ)	нра́ви+ ся	вы́гляде+
infinitive	грустить	нра́виться	вы́глядеть
non-past			
я	грущу́	нра́влюсь	вы́гляжу
ты	грусти́шь	нра́вишься	вы́глядишь
он,она́, оно́	грусти́т	нра́вится	вы́глядит
мы	грусти́м	нра́вимся	вы́глядим
вы	грусти́те	нра́витесь	вы́глядите
они́	грустя́т	нра́вятся	вы́глядят
p a s t			
он	грусти́л	нра́вился	вы́глядел
она́	грусти́ла	нра́вилась	вы́глядела
они́	грусти́ли	нра́вились	вы́глядели

4.2c

1. выглядит
2. взглядом
3. На мой взгляд
4. наглядно

4.5d

1. роста
2. растения
3. растёт
4. взрослых
5. взрослые
6. возраста

4.6 for stress patterns see Appendix

stress pattern C	един.	множ
им.		во́лосы
вин		во́лосы
род		воло́с
дат		волоса́м
пред		о волоса́х
твор		волоса́ми

stress: AC	един.	множ
им.	у́хо	у́ши
вин	у́хо	у́ши
род	у́ха	уше́й
дат	у́ху	уша́м
пред	об у́хе	об уша́х
твор	у́хом	уша́ми

stress pattern AB	един.	множ
им.	нос	носы́
вин	нос	носы́
род	но́са	носо́в
дат	но́су	носа́м
пред	о но́се/в носу́	о носа́х
твор	но́сом	носа́ми

AB	един.	множ
им.	глаз	глаза́
вин	глаз	глаза́
род	гла́за	глаз
дат	гла́зу	глаза́м
пред	о гла́зе/в глазу́	о глаза́х
твор	гла́зом	глаза́ми

BC	един.	множ
им.	губа́	гу́бы
вин	губу́	гу́бы
род	губы́	губ
дат	губе́	губа́м
пред	о губе́	губа́х
твор	губо́й	губа́ми

AC	един.	множ
им.	зуб	зу́бы
вин	зуб	зу́бы
род	зу́ба	зубо́в
дат	зу́бу	зуба́м
пред	о зубе	о зуба́х
твор	зу́бом	зуба́ми

4.8

1. Линда похожа на (свою) подругу.
2. Брат похож на сестру.
3. Борис похож на Сашу
4. Нина похожа на Вадима
5. Иван похож на Анну.
6. Вика похожа на Джона.

4.9

1. Нет, он не похож на него. Они не похожи друг на друга.
2. Нет, она не похожа на неё. Они не похожи друг на друга.
3. Нет он не похож на неё. Они не похожи друг на друга.
4. Нет, он не похож на него. Они не похожи друг на друга.
5. Нет, она не похожа на неё. Они не похожи друг на друга.

4.10

1. У него были умные глаза.
3. У неё были тонкие руки, были крацивые длинные пальцы.
6. У него была седая борода, были длинные седые волосы.

4.11

1. Это был высокий человек с чёрными волосами.
3. Официант был полный, с длиннами усами.
5. На диване сидел котёнок с зелённами глазами.

4.15

1. .... в коричневой куртке
2. ... в розовом платье
3. ... в чёрном длинном пальто
4. ... в красном купальнике
5. ... в спортивном костюме
6. ... белом халате
7. ... в синем плаще
8. ... в сером костюме
9. ... в тёмных очках и чёрной шляпе
10. ... в кроссовках и джинсах

4.16

1. в клетку
2. в полоску
3. в клетку
4. в горошек
5. в красный горошек
6. в клетку

4.18a

1. Она обычно ходит в коротких юбках.
2. Она никогда не ходит в брюках
3. Он всегда ходит в спортивном костюме.
4. Он никогда не ходит в галстуке

4.18b

1. Я люблю носить кроссовки.
2. Он часто носит чёрный костюм.
3. Он никогда не носит джинсы
4. Она всегда носит красную куртку.

4.21

1. нравишься
2. понравилось, нравится
3. нравятся, нравлюсь
4. нравились, понравилась
5. нравилась, понравилась
6. нравятся

4.23.c
1. открыть
2. закройте
3. на открытии, на открытии
4. открытие
5. крыши
6. открывалку, открыть

4.26
1. не надевать
2. не покупать
3. не брать
4. не покупать
5. не надевать
6. не делать
7. не рассказывать

4.27
купить, покупать, взять, не брать, полететь, лететь

4.29
1. Антону не надо покупать плавки. Сергею надо купить плавки.
2. Лене надо купить купальник. Тане не надо покупать купальника.
3. Мне не надо покупать плащ. Ему надо купить плащ.
4. Брату надо купить тёплую куртку. Мне не надо покупать куртки.

1. Мне не надо готовить перевода. Олегу надо приготовить перевод.
2. Свете надо приготовить текст... Мише не надо готовить...
3. Ольге не надо готовить график. Саше надо приготовить график.
4. Мне не надо готовить программу семинара. Ей надо приготовить ...

4.30
1. Маме не надо готовить обед. Она уже приготовила.
2. Павлу не надо переводить текст. Он уже перевёл.
3. Нине не надо писать домашнее задание. Она уже написала.
4. Нам не надо составлять программу. Уже составили.
5. Мне не надо делать работу. Я уже сделала.

4.31
1. уходил
2. пришли
3. уезжала
4. уехал
5. уезжал
6. взял
7. отдавал, принёс
8. включили

4.32

1. сам   самому
2. сама   самой
3. сами   самим
4. сами   самим
5. сам(а) самому (самой)
6. сама   самой.

4.33

Вчера вечером звонил приятель моего друга Андрея. Я познакомился с Андреем когда я был в Москве. Брат Андрея, Сергей, только что прилетел из Москвы. Он привёз мне письмо от Андрея. Мы с Сергеем договорились встретиться сегодня вечером около метро.

Я стою сейчас у входа в метро, и я немного волнуюсь. Как я его узнаю. Вот идёт молодой человек в голубой рубашке и джинсах. Сергей сказал, что он будет носить голубую рубашку и джинсы. Может быть это он, но он проходит мимо меня. Высокий брюнет стоит недалеко от входа в метро. Он тоже носит джинсы и голубую рубашку. Я подхожу к нему и спрашиваю, «Вы не Сергей?». Он смотрит на меня и не понимает. А вот спешит молодой человек, брюнет, среднего роста, в джинсах и голубой рубашке. Я знаю, что это Сергей потому, что он очень похож на Андрея.

4.36

	един.	множ.
им.	лицо́	ли́ца
вин.	лицо	ли́ца
род.	лица́	ли́ц
дат.	лицу́	ли́цам
пред.	о лице́	о ли́цах
твор.	лицо́м	ли́цами

	един.	множ.
им.	ше́я	ше́и
вин.	ше́ю	ше́и
род.	ше́и	ше́й
дат.	ше́е	ше́ям
пред.	о ше́е	о ше́ях
твор.	ше́ей	ше́ями

4.37.d

1. спросил
2. попросил
3. попрошу
4. попросила (просит, попросит), спросить
5. Спроси́
6. спрашивает
7. Попроси́
8. попросила
9. спрашивает
10. попросил
11. спросил/а
12. спросила
13. попросила
14. попросил/а

4.38

1. видный
2. видно
3. свидетель
4. увидел/а
5. вижу
6. вид
7. видит
8. Видимо

Глаголы четвёртого урока.

stem	взять	бр/а	открывай+	открой+
infinitive	взять	брать	открыва́ть	открыть
non-past				
я	возьму́	беру́	открыва́ю	откро́ю
ты	возьмёшь	берёшь	открыва́ешь	откро́ешь
он,она́, оно́	возьмёт	берёт	открыва́ет	откро́ет
мы	возьмём	берём	открыва́ем	откро́ем
вы	возьмёте	берёте	открыва́ете	откро́ете
они́	возьмут	беру́т	открыва́ют	откро́ют
past				
он	взял	брал	открыва́л	откры́л
она́	взяла́	брала́	открыва́ла	откры́ла
они́	взя́ли	бра́ли	открыва́ли	откры́ли

stem	покупа́й+	купи́+	проси́+	попроси́+
infinitive	покупа́ть	купи́ть	проси́ть	попроси́ть
non-past				
я	покупа́ю	куплю́	прошу́	попрошу́
ты	покупа́ешь	ку́пишь	про́сишь	попро́сишь
он, она́, оно́	покупа́ет	ку́пит	про́сит	попро́сит
мы	покупа́ем	ку́пим	про́сим	попро́сим
вы	покупа́ете	ку́пите	про́сите	попро́сите
они́	покупа́ют	ку́пят	про́сят	попро́сят
past				
он	покупа́л	купи́л	проси́л	попроси́л
она́	покупа́ла	купи́ла	проси́ла	попроси́ла
они́	покупа́ли	купи́ли	проси́ли	попроси́ли

stem	гото́ви+	пригото́ви+	спра́шивай+	спроси́+
infinitive	гото́вить	пригото́вить	спра́шивать	спроси́ть
non-past				
я	гото́влю	пригото́влю	спра́шиваю	спрошу́
ты	гото́вишь	пригото́вишь	спра́шиваешь	спро́сишь
он, она́, оно́	гото́вит	пригото́вит	спра́шивает	спро́сит
мы	гото́вим	пригото́вим	спра́шиваем	спро́сим
вы	гото́вите	пригото́вите	спра́шиваете	спро́сите
они́	гото́вят	пригото́вят	спра́шивают	спро́сят
past				
он	гото́вил	пригото́вил	спра́шивал	спроси́л
она́	гото́вила	пригото́вила	спра́шивала	спроси́ла
они́	гото́вили	пригото́вили	спра́шивали	спроси́ли

Урок 5:   Письменные задания

5.1
преподаёт
издаёт
продаёт
продаёт

1. подарили
2. одарённый
3. дарят, подарки
4. поблагодарила

5.4.с
1. верила
2. верю
3. верит, верующий
4. наверное
7. верит

5.5

	един.	множ.
им.	ценá	цéны
вин.	цéну	цéны
род.	цены́	цéн
дат.	ценé	цéнам
пред.	о ценé	цéнах
твор.	ценóй	цéнами

	един.	множ.
им.	водá	вóды
вин.	вóду	вóды
род.	воды́	вод
дат.	водé	вóдам
пред.	о водé	вóдах
твор.	водой	вóдами

	един.	множ.
им.	рубль	рубли́
вин.	рубль	рубли́
род.	рубля́	рублéй
дат.	рублé	рубля́м
пред.	о рублé	о рубля́х
твор.	рублём	рубля́ми

93

fleeting (e)	един.	множ.
им.	копе́йка	копе́йки
вин.	копе́йку	копе́йки
род.	копе́йки	копе́ек
дат.	копе́йке	копе́йкам
пред.	о копе́йке	о копе́йках
твор.	копе́йкой	копе́йками

5.8с
1. цены
2. оценки
3. оцениваем
5. драгоценности
6. бесценно

5.9а
1 Магазин открывается...
2. Библиотека закрывается...
3. Новый магазин строится
4. Красная икра продаётся в этом магазине
5. Киоск закрывается...
6. Большая распродажа обуви начинается ...
7. Распродажа детских игрушек заканчивается.

б
1. В нашем районе строят новую школу.
2. Закрывают библиотеку сегодня в шесть часов.
3. В этой кондитерской продают вкусные пирожные.
4. На первом курсе изучают русскую литературу
8. Скоро здесь откроют новую станцию метро.

5.10
дава́й	дай	пока́зывай
покажи́	зака́зывай	закажи́
смотри́	посмотри́	бери́
возьми́	покупа́й	купи́
сове́туй	посове́туй	дари́
подари́	выбира́й	вы́бери
плати́	заплати́	налива́й
нале́й	объясня́й	объясни́
завора́чивай	заверни́	помога́й
помоги́	пе́й	вы́пей.

5.11
1. Дай
2. посмотри
3. подари
4. заплатите
5. купи
6. посоветуй
7. возьми

5.12.с
1.заплачу
2. бесплатная, платить
3. зарплаты до зарплаты
4. бесплатно.

5.13.с
1. Посоветуй
2. совет
3. ответ
4. ответь
5. безответственно
6. Привет

5.14
1. Покажите её
2.подари́ ей их
3. вы́бери его
4. заплати за них
5. посмотри́ её
6. скажи ему об этом
7. запиши его
8. позвони ему

5.15

Positive degree	Adverb	Simple Comparative
свéжий	свéжо	свежéе
вкýсно	вкýсно	вкуснéе
красúво	красúво	красúвее
дёшево	дёшево	дешéвле
дорóгой	дорóгой	дорóже
слáдкий	слáдкий	слáще
		No mutation, full "ee" ending:
весёлый	вéсело	веселéе
бы́стый	бы́стро	быстрée
мéдленный	мéдленно	мéдленнее
свéтый	светлó	светлée
тёмый	темнó	темнée
трýдый	трýдно	труднée
вáжый	вáжно	важнée
интересый	интерéсно	интерéснее
		ONE LETTER Mutation:
дорогóй	дóрого	дорóже
грóмкий	грóмко	грóмче
тúхий	тúхо	тúше
богáтый	богáто	богáче
		More than one letter mutation
дешёвый	дёшево	дешéвле
блúзкий	блúзко	блúже
далёкий	далекó	дáльше
сладкий	сладко	слáще
		From different roots
хорóший	хорошó	лýчше
плохóй	плóхо	хýже
мáленький	мало	мéньше
большóй	много	бóльше

5.17а

1 вкуснée
2. дорóже
3. бóльше
4. мéньше
5. свежée
6. дешéвле
7. тúше
8. красúвее
9.лýчше
10. слáще

б.

1. лучше
2. мéдленнее
3. быстрée
4. грóмче
5. лучше

6. доро́же
7. деше́вле
8. краси́вее
9. бо́льше
10. ме́ньше

Глаголы пятого урока

stem	плати+	сто́и+	дари+	заказывай+	заказа́+	сове́това+
infinitive	плати́ть	сто́ить	дари́ть	заказыва	заказа́ть	сове́товать
non-past						
я	плачу́	сто́ю	дарю́	зака́зываю	закажу́	сове́тую
ты	пла́тишь	сто́ишь	да́ришь	зака́зываешь	зака́жешь	сове́туешь
он,она́,оно́	пла́тит	сто́ит	да́рит	зака́зывает	зака́жет	сове́тует
мы	пла́тим	сто́им	да́рим	зака́зываем	зака́жем	сове́туем
вы	пла́тите	сто́ите	да́рите	зака́зываете	зака́жете	сове́туете
они́	пла́тят	сто́ят	да́рят	зака́зывают	зака́жут	сове́туют
past						
он	плати́л	сто́ил	дари́л	зака́зывал	заказа́л	сове́товал
она́	плати́ла	сто́ила	дари́ла	зака́зывала	заказа́ла	сове́товала
они́	плати́ли	сто́или	дари́ли	зака́зывали	заказа́ли	сове́товали

5.22
1. Не ходи
2. не заходи
3. не плати
4. не говори
5. не покупай
6. не отвечай
7. не открывай
8. не гуляй
9. не заворачивай
10. не спрашивай
11. не звони
12. не забывай
13. не показывай

5.23
1. не ходи
2. не закрывай
3. не открывай
4. не спрашивай
5. не помогай мне
6. не покупай
7. не заворачивай
8. не дари
9. не готовь
10. не показывай
11. не говори
12. не рассказывай

5.30
1. Я **ничего не** забыла
2. Мы **никому не** звонили.
3. Мы **ни о чём не** узнали.
4. Я **ни в чём не** виноват.
5. Мы **ничего не** купили.

6. Он **ни с кем не** дружит.

7. Они **нигде не** были.

8. Мы **никому не** дарили цветы.

9. Мы **ни у кого не** спрашивали, где рынок.

10. **Никто не** пришёл вовремя.

11. **Никому не** было весело.

12. **Нигде** ему **не** нравится.

5.31

1. Мы ни о чём не говорили

2. Он ни с кем не говорил

3. Мы ни о ком не думали.

4. Я ничего не брал.

5. Нигде не было чёрной икры.

6. Я никуда не пойду сегодня вечером

7. Я никому не звонила.

8. Никто не знает, когда она придёт.

9. Мы нé были ни у кого.

10. Я вчера никуда не ходила.

5.32

а. —Сколько у тебя денег?

— Десять рублей

— И ты хочешь купить подарок?

—Да

—На десять рублей ничего нельзя купить. Всё намного (гораздо) дороже.

б.—Не покупай эту коробку конфет. Она дорогая, и эти конфеты не очень вкусные.

—А что тогда купить? (Что мне тогда купить?)

—Купи торт.

—Какой, шоколадный?

—Нет, фруктовый. Можно купить очень вкусный фруктовый торт в булочной, напротив. (через улицу)

5.33

Я сегодня ходил по магазинам потому, что мне надо купить подарки матери (маме), отцу (папе), брату, сестре и друзьям. Я купила матери красивый платок в магазине «Русские Сувениры». Он стоил тысячу двести пятьдесят два рубля. Брату я купил плакаты в книжном магазине. Они были не дорогие—стоили десять рублей сорок восемь копеек. Я долго решал, что купить отцу, но, наконец, я решил купить ему красный галстук. Я хотел купить сестре палехскую шкатулку, но все шкатулки были очень дорогие, и продавец (продавщица) посоветовал(а) мне купить ей матрёшку. Я думаю, что всем понравятся эти подарки.

5.37.с

1. появился

2. объявил

3. объявление

5.41

На Тверской улице в Москве и на Невском проспекте в Петербурге находятся два магазина, которые называются «Елисеевский». Григорий Елисеев открыл эти магазины в начале двадцатого века. Магазины очень красивые. В них высокие зекала́, замечательные прилавки, много разных отделов. Есть кондитерская, мясной отдел, молочный отдел, рыбный отдел, отдел овощи и фрукты, винный отдел. Самые хорошие и свежие продукты всегда продаются в этих магазинах. В рыбном отделе можно купить чёрную и красную икру, большой ассортимент селёдки, белой и красной рыбы. В кондитерской можно купить вкусные пироженые, шоколад, красивые коборки конфет. В Киеве тоже есть магазин «Елисеевский». Эти магазины самые знаменитые в России.

5.42

Do not use a dictionary!!! Use words and phrases that you know or that you know you should know from this chapter, and others that you know or should know from earlier chapters. You might use some of the following, for instance:

собираться/собраться (поехать куда-нибудь на праздник, на каникулы)
покупать/купить подарки кому-нибудь
ходить по магазинам
дорогие, дешёвые подарки
дарить/подарить кому-нибудь
получить подарки от кого-нибудь

Глаголы шестого урока

stem	стоя́+	ста́ви+	лежа́+	клад+	положи́+
infinitive	стоя́ть	ста́вить	лежа́ть	класть	положи́ть
non-past					
я	стою́	ста́влю	лежу́	кладу́	положу́
ты	стои́шь	ста́вишь	лежи́шь	кладёшь	поло́жишь
он,она́,оно́	стои́т	ста́вит	лежи́т	кладёт	поло́жит
мы	стои́м	ста́вим	лежи́м	кладём	поло́жим
вы	стои́те	ста́вите	лежи́те	кладёте	поло́жите
они́	стоя́т	ста́вят	лежа́т	кладу́т	поло́жат
past					
он	стоя́л	ста́вил	лежа́л	кла́л	положи́л
она́	стоя́ла	ста́вила	лежа́ла	кла́ла	положи́ла
они́	стоя́ли	ста́вили	лежа́ли	кла́ли	положи́ли
imperative	сто́й	ставь(те)	лежи́(те)	клади́(те)	положи́(те)

stem	сиде́+	сажа́й+	посади́+	висе́+	ве́шай+
infinitive	сиде́ть	сажа́ть	посади́ть	висе́ть	ве́шать
non-past					
я	сижу́	сажа́ю	посажу́	вишу́	ве́шаю
ты	сиди́шь	сажа́ешь	поса́дишь	виси́шь	ве́шаешь
он,она́,оно́	сиди́т	сажа́ет	поса́дит	виси́т	ве́шает
мы	сиди́м	сажа́ем	поса́дим	виси́м	ве́шаем
вы	сиди́те	сажа́ете	поса́дите	виси́те	ве́шаете
они́	сидя́т	сажа́ют	поса́дят	вися́т	ве́шают
past					
он	сиде́л	сажа́л	посади́л	висе́л	ве́шал
она́	сиде́ла	сажа́ла	посади́ла	висе́ла	ве́шала
они́	сиде́ли	сажа́ли	посади́ли	висе́ли	ве́шали
imperative	сиди́(те)	сажай(те)	посади́(те)	виси́(те)	ве́шай(те)

6.3

This exercise is intended to reinforce your understanding of the numbers as subjects and direct objects and the nouns that follow them.

The noun стул has unusual plural forms: сту́лья(nom. acc.), сту́льев (gen), сту́льям(dat.), о сту́льях(prep.), сту́льями(inst). игрушка has a fleeting -e which we see in the gen. plural игру́шек. Learn these forms.

а.

комнаты, стульев, кресла, полки, картин, окна, картины, игрушек, шкафа, полки

б.

столов, стулья, плакатов, полки.

6.5

This exercise reinforces the present tense conjugations of the intransitive verbs of position.

а. стоя́т, стои́т

б. лежа́т, лежи́т

ц. вися́т, вися́т, виси́т

д. сиди́т, сидя́т, сидя́т.

6.8

This exercise reinforces your command of the transitive and intransitive verbs, and some practice forming the prepositional and accusative. Remember that the intransitive will use **в/на** and the prepositional. The transitive verbs will take the same prepositions but use the accusative after them.

1. Оно стои́т на пра́здничном столе́.

Она положи́ла его на пра́здничный стол.

2. Оно лежит в холодильнике

Я положила его в холодильник

3. Я его вешаю в шкаф

Оно висит в шкафу́.

4. Я положил их на верхнюю полку.

Они лежат на верхней полке.

5. Они стоят в большой красивой вазе.

Я поставил их в большую красивую вазу.

6.9

This exercise is meant to reinforce the concepts of position and positioning. The questions will begin with either **куда** or **где**. Answer the questions in full sentences.

1. Куда вы поставили цветы?

2. Где лежат вилки?

3. Куда он положил вилки?

4. Где висит фотография?

5. Куда она повесила фотографию?

6. Где стои́т пиво?

7. Куда вы поставили пиво?

6.10

This exercise requires you to distinguish between context that require a transitive verb and those that require an intransitive one. The exercise also requires that you distinguish between the perfective and imperfective use of the transitive verbs.

a. стоя́т, стоя́т, ста́вите, ста́влю ... на стол, поставили, поставил

b. лежит, лежит, кладёте, кладу на полку, положили, положил

c. висит, висит, вешаете, вешаю в шкаф, повесили, повесил

d. сидит, сидит, сажаете, сажаю, посадите (сажаете), посажу (сажаю)

6.11

This exercises covers the forms of стол and стул. The prepositions вокруг, посредине, require the genitive. To take a seat at a table is сесть за стол (за + accus.) To be seated at the table is сидеть за столóм (за+instr.)

a. стол, стола, стулья, столе, стола, стол, столом, стульев, стул.

6.14

Numbers and the genitive, and vocabulary practice.

a. прибора, вилки, ножа, ложки, тарелки, стакана.

б. 1. Стол был накрыт на пять приборов: на столе лежало пять вилок, пять ножей, пять ложек, пять тарелок, пять стаканов.

2. Стол был накрыт на один прибор: на столе лежала одна вилка, один нож, одна ложка, одна тарелка, один стакан.

6.16, 6.17

Practice with the instrumental of nouns and interrogatives after the preposition "c" and food words. In addition in 17 we practice contrasting the use of the instrumental with and without a preposition and get some practice conjugating useful verbs.

6.16

1. с маслом, с сыром
2. с капустой
3. с рисом
4. с грибами
5. с картошкой
6. с пирожком
7. с колбасой

6.17

1. С чем вы едите борщ?
2. Чем вы чистите зубы?
3. С чем вы пьёте кофе?
4. Чем она пишет в тетради?
5. Чем преподаватель исправляет ошибки?
6. С чем вы будете есть (ты будешь есть) макароны?
7. С чем этот торт?
8. С чем эта бутылка.

6.18

See above for discussion of these particles.

1. что-**нибудь**, что-**то**
2. кто-**нибудь**, кто-**то**
3. что-**нибудь**, какая-**то**
4. кто-**нибудь**, какой-**то**
5. куда-**нибудь**, куда-**то**
6. что-**нибудь**, что-**то**
7. что-**нибудь**, Да, мы ели что-**то**.
8. что-**нибудь**, что-**то**
9. что-**нибудь**, что-**то**
10. что-**нибудь**, что-**то**
11. кто-**нибудь**, кто-**то**
12. что-**нибудь**, что-**то**
13. что-**нибудь**, что-**то**

6.19d

1. ходить в гости, гости
2. гостеприимство
3. угощайтесь, пожалуйста
4. гостиной

6.20

1. гости
2. гостей
3. гостям (We were happy to have guests)
4. гостей (We treated our guests to tasty meat pies)
5. гостями
6. гостях

6.21&25

stem	сади́+ся	сесть
infinitive	сади́ться	сесть
non-past		
я	сажу́сь	ся́ду
ты	сади́шься	ся́дешь
он, она́, оно́	сади́тся	ся́дет
мы	сади́мся	ся́дем
вы	сади́тесь	ся́дете
они́	садя́тся	ся́дут
past		
он	сади́лся	сел
она́	сади́лась	села
они́	сади́лись	сели

6.22

1. Да, давайте пить...
2. Да, давайте готовить...
3. Да, давайте танцевать...
4. Да, давайте смотреть...
5. Да, давайте делать...

6.23

1. Давайте вы́пьем пива (the genitive here means "some" beer)
2. Давайте посмотрим
3. Давайте погуляем
4. Давайте приготовим
5. Давайте купим
6. Давайте попробуем
7. Давайте поспим
8. Давайте накроем
9. Давайте пойдём
10. Давайте пригласим
11. Давайте позвоним и позовём

6.24

1. позвоним
2. позвонит
3. напишем
4. поедем
5. напишет
6. поедет
7. поможет
8. поможем
9. попросим
10. попросит
11. купим
12. купит

6.25

stem	пёк+/испёк+
infinitive	ис/печь
non-past	
я	ис/пеку́
ты	ис/печёшь
он, она́, оно́	ис/печёт
мы	ис/печём
вы	ис/печёте
они́	ис/пеку́т
p a s t	
он	ис/пёк
она́	ис/пекла́
они́	ис/пекли́

6.26

запечёное мясо   пекла   печенье
пекарне   печь

Ex. 27, 28 and 29 reinforce the use of the construction "пора" in the present and the past. The word "пора" does **not**, in and of itself force the imperfective infinitive to follow, however, in all the contexts here the imperfective must be used. It is very often the case that **пора** implies "it is time to start to do something," and so **пора** is often followed by an imperfective infinitive.

6.27

1.Нам пора работать
2. Им пора отдыхать
3. Вам пора обедать
4. Тебе пора вставать,
5. Мне пора выходить
6. Ей пора ложиться
7. Ему пора накрывать ...
8. Нам пора печь

6.28

1. Ей пора было ...
2. Им пора было ...
3. Ему пора было
4. Тебе пора было
5. Нам пора было
6. Вам пора было
7. Мне пора было

6.30

б. 1.Мы с Таней	Мы с ней
2. Мы с Олегом	Мы с ним
3. Мы с Линдой	Мы с ней
4. Мы с Сашей	Мы с ней (с ним)
5. Мы с Ниной	Мы с ней

с

1. Вы с Ларисой	Вы с ней
2. Вы с Наташей	Вы с ней
3. Вы с Николаем	Вы с ним
4.Вы с Антоном	Вы с ним
5. Вы с Джоном	Вы с ним

6.31.a

1. Нам с Сашей	Нам с ней
2. Нам с Борисом	Нам с ним
3. Нам с Кристиной	Нам с ней
4. Нам с Леной	Нам с ней
5. Нам с Андреем	Нам с ним

6.31.б

1. Вам с Зиной	Вам с ней
2. Вам с Иваном	Вам с ним
3. Вам с Мариной	Вам с ним
4. Вам со Стивом	Вам с ним
5. Вам с Аней	Вам с ней

6.33

See the discussion of this point on PT-12, ex. 35.3. "**чтобы**" clauses are a bit of a problem in Russian because in English we don't really need to use a complex sentence to express desire or command. With some verbs we can really only use a direct object and an infinitive: "He wants them to buy his book." We can't really say in English, "He wants that they buy his book." We can, however, say both "He asked us to buy his book" and "He asked that we buy his book." In other words, in English there are cases when you can use only the simple form and others where either the simple or complex form will do. There are not, it seems, cases where you can use only the complex form. In Russian it is the other way around. There are some cases where you can use a direct object and an infinitve or a **чтобы** clause with equal confidence, but there are not cases where you can use only an object and an infinitive. This is well and fine and great to know. What you need to learn here is that the verb "**попросить**" is one of the verbs that can be used in constructions that seem to parallel both English constructions. That is, you can say either, "Он попросил **меня купить** книгу." or "Он попросил, чтобы я купил книгу." [Unfortunately, our favorite frequent verb хотеть is one of those "verbs of volition" that cannot use either construction. You can only say, "Я хочу, чтобы ты купил книгу"— but that's a different exercise]. **Чтобы** clauses, when the subject of the "clause of purpose" (the one after the main clause, the one where we find out the purpose of the action of the main clause) is different from that of the main clause are formed by **чтобы** and the past tense of the verb (which agrees, of course, with the subject of the "clause of purpose"). For those of you who are "clause-trophobic" work through the exercise and see if you can fit the explanation to the pattern enough times to understand it.

6.33

1. Он попросил маму положить ему салат.
Он попросил, чтобы мама положила ему салат.
2. Наташа попросила его передать ей соль.
Наташа попросила, чтобы он передал ей соль.
3. Бабушка попросила внука помочь ей повесить картину.
Бабушка попросила, чтобы внук помог ей повесить картину.
4.Брат попросил сестру приготовить сегодня ужин.
Брат попросил, чтобы сестра приготовила сегодня ужин.
5.Марина попросила официанта принести ещё кофе.
Марина попросила, чтобы официант принёс ещё кофе.

6.37

1. Девушка, которая заказывала французское вино
2. Французское вино, которое заказывает девушка, очень вкусное
3. Официант принёс французское вино, которое заказала девушка.
1. Мама, которая накрывает на стол, просит меня помочь ей.
2. Хозяйка, которая накрыла на стол, позвала всех к столу
3. Стол, который мама накрывает, почти готов.
4. Стол, который хозяйка накрыла, выглядел празднично.

1. Мальчик, который читает книгу, не хочет идти обедать.
2. Мальчик, который читал книгу, не слышал...
3. Книга, которую читает мальчик, очень интересная.
4. Книга, которую мальчик прочитал, лежит на полке.

Урок 7: Письменные задания

глаголы

stem	аплодирова+	стара́й+ся	выбирай+	выб/ра+
infinitive	аплодировать	стараться	выбира́ть	вы́брать
non-past				
я	аплоди́рую	стара́юсь	выбира́ю	вы́беру
ты	аплоди́руешь	стара́ешься	выбира́ешь	вы́берешь
он, она́, оно́	аплоди́рует	стара́ется	выбира́ет	вы́берет
мы	аплоди́руем	стара́емся	выбира́ем	вы́берем
вы	аплоди́руете	стара́етесь	выбира́ете	вы́берете
они́	аплоди́руют	стара́ются	выбира́ют	вы́берут
past				
он	аплоди́ровал	стара́лся	выбира́л	вы́брал
она́	аплоди́ровала	стара́лась	выбира́ла	вы́брала
они́	аплоди́ровали	стара́лись	выбира́ли	вы́брали
imperative	аплоди́руй	стара́йся	выбира́й(те)	вы́берите

им	геро́й	музе́й	исто́рия	галере́я
вин	геро́я	музе́й	исто́рию	галере́ю
род	геро́я	музе́я	исто́рии	галере́и
дат	геро́ю	музе́ю	исто́рии	галере́е
пред	о геро́е	о музе́е	исто́рии	галере́е
твор	геро́ем	музе́ем	исто́рией	галере́ей
им	геро́и	музе́и	исто́рии	галере́и
вин	геро́ев	музе́и	исто́рии	галере́и
род	геро́ев	музе́ев	исто́рий	галере́й
дат	геро́ям	музе́ям	исто́риям	галере́ям
пред	о геро́ях	музе́ях	исто́риях	галере́ях
твор	геро́ями	музе́ями	исто́риями	галере́ями

7.1d

1. точки зрения, постановка
2. выставочном зале, выставка
3. достать
4. зрители
5. зрительный зал.

7.6
1. по роману ...
по искусству
3. по пьесе ...
4. по роману
5. по русскому языку
6. по химии
7. по роману...
8. по истории...
9. по математике
10. по истории искусства
11. по истории театра

7.8.
1. Какой спектакль вы смотрели?
2. В каком музее вы были вчера?
3. На какую выставку вы ходили?
4. В какой музей вы пойдёте завтра?
5. На какую выставку вы ходили?
6. Какую работу вы писали?
7. Какой семинар он ведёт?
8. Какая лекция была утром?

7.10
1.Нет, к сожалению, он не смог его достать.
2. ..., мы не смогли её достать.
3. ... мы не смогли их достать.
4. ..., она не смогла его достать.
5. ..., мы не смогли их достать.

7.13
1. которую
2. которым
3. котором
4. которую
5. которым
6. которой
7. которой
8. который
9. котором
10. которые

7.15
1...., в котором участвовали...
2. ..., о которой была статья ...
3. ..., о котором я вам говорила.
4. ..., которого я слышал на концерте.
5. ..., у которого мы были вчера в мастерской.
6. ..., с которыми мы ходили в Национальную галерею.
7. ..., в котором жил Достоевский.
8. ..., о которых вы мне говорили.
9. ..., который выступает в Старом цирке.

7.17

Наши друзья, которые очень любят театр, пригласили нас пойти с ними в новый экпериментальный театр-студию. Этот театр, в котором играют молодые талантливые артисты сейчас очень популярен. Мы посмотрели пьесу, написанную молодым драматургом, (которую написал молодой драматург). Нам всем очень понравилась постановка, которую поставил главный режиссёр театра. После спектакля мы говорили обо всех артистах, но особенно об артисте, который играл главную роль. Этот талантливый актёр, который раньше жил в Петербурге, сейчас живёт и работает в Москве.

7.18

1.Да, она очень довольна нашим вечером. 2. Да, он очень доволен выставкой. 3. Да, они очень довольны экскурсией. 4. Да, я очень доволен/довольна ролью. 5. Да, она очень довольна моим подарком. 6. Да, они очень довольны этим курсом.

7.19

1.. Мама довольна детьми? Да, она ими довольна. 4. Сергей доволен своей поездкой? Да, он ей доволен.

7.20

1. Линда довольна тем, что выбрала курс по истории русского театра. 3. Мы довольны тем, что участвовали в концерте.

7.22.

учится, занимается, изучает, изучает, учит, научился, учил, занимается.

7.24

1.На самый популярный, 2. о самом интересном художнике 3. Мой самый любимый актёр 4. с самым известным драматургом. 5. В самом маленьком зале 6. В самом дорогом ресторане. 7. В самой старой части города

7.27 The formation of short-form verbal adjectives, (past passive):

Their formation is complex, but this form is quite common in conversational Russian. You will probably learn more of them by engaging in and listening to conversation than by memorizing the rules for their formation, and you are already familiar or at least can recognize quite a few of them. Nevertheless, a summary of the rules is as follows:

There are three suffixes: -т-, -ён-, -н-.

Add -т-

to suffixless stems that end in

р (none in this course, but one useful one is за́перт, заперта́ "locked")

м (the one to remember here is я за́нят(а́)-I am busy),

н (чн+, оден+. These are the most common stems in this category. You should recognize them as the stems for the infinitives нача́ть, оде́ть. The past passive verbal adjectives will be на́чат, оде́т,

й (мой+, крой+. There are only a few of these stems, but these two are very common. You should recognize them as the stems that produce the infinitives мыть, крыть and form the verbs умы́ться, откры́ть, закры́ть). The past passive verbal adjectives will be имыт, закры́т.

в (забыв+) забы́т (forgotten), is the one not to forget.

to suffixed stems in o- (нако́лот—"speared, pinned, fastened, tatooed"—none to worry about in this course)

to suffixed stems in ну- (quite a few verbs—поки́нут—"abandonded", but none to worry about quite yet)

Add ён- to stems in

unsuffixed д, перевёд+ gives переведён
unsuffixed с, (нёс+ gives несён)
unsuffixed т, (none in this course)
unsuffixed г, (none in this course)
unsuffixed к, испёк+ gives испечён (baked)
unsuffixed б, (none in this course)
unsuffixed п, (none in this course)
and the suffix -и-, подари+ gives пода́рен, купи+ gives ку́плен,
утоми+ gives утомлён—see note below on mutation

Add н- to other stems—there are lots

stress and mutation are as follows with the following suffixes:

т stress as in past masculine

ён stress shifts to the left if shifting in present

н stress shifts to left for all post root stressed stems

mutations occur in many forms—Remember that before -e, ст mutates into щ; п, б, в > пл, бл, вл; з, г >ж and к,т > ч.

For this course you need to recognize the form and recognize what verb it comes from.

7.28

Московский университет основал Михаил Васильевич Ломоносов. 2. Булгаков написал роман «Мастер и Маргарита» в конце тридцатых годов. 3. Братья Третьяковы создали Третьяковскую галерею. 4. Архитектор Казаков построил это здание. 5. Мой знакомый художник нарисовал эту картину.

7.29

а. 1. В следующем году организуют семинар по истории русского театра. 2. Скоро переведут рассказы этого писателя на английский язык. 3. Здесь построят театр. 4. В конце этого месяца закроют музей.
б. В прошлом году в нашем городе открыли ещё один театр. 2. Недавно издали письма Марины Цветаевой. 3. На прошлой неделе организовали экскурсию в Эрмитаж. 4. Эту картину купила моя подруга.

7.34

1. интересный, интересен 2. известен, известный. 3. великолепная, великолепна 4. сложная, сложна 5. простой, прост.
35.1. сложно 2. талантливо 3. прекрасно 4. интересно 5. просто. 6. непонятно 7. выразительно

stem	обижа́й+	оби́де+
infinitive	обижа́ть	оби́деть
non-past		
я	обижа́ю	оби́жу
ты	обижа́ешь	оби́дишь
он, она́, оно́	обижа́ет	оби́дит
мы	обижа́ем	оби́дим
вы	обижа́ете	оби́дите
они́	обижа́ют	оби́дят
past		
он	обижа́л	оби́дел
она́	обижа́ла	оби́дела
они́	обижа́ли	оби́дели

7.39

1. обидел, обидела
2. обижается, обижает
3. обижайся, обидите
4. обижается, обижать

   From this little exercise you can notice that the verb **обижать(ся)/обидеть(ся)** is used in contexts where the simple "to insult" doesn't work. The verb is used more frequently in Russian that its translation would lead us to believe. See if you can translate these sentences into good English if you have time.

7.40

—Джон, что вы собираетесь делать сегодня вечером?

—Ничего, я свободен сегодня вечером, а что?

—Давай пойдём в кино.

—С удовольствием. Что ты хочешь посмотреть?

—Я хочу посмотреть новый детектив, но не знаю, где он идёт.

—Я знаю, он идёт в «Форуме».

—Отлично, давай встретимся в семь часов.

—Хорошо, где?

—В ресторане рядом с кинотеатром.

—Договорились

7.41

Double underline means you should know or learn fast these construction.

Я уже давно хочу пойти на спектакль в театре на Бродвее, но очень трудно достать билеты, и они очень дорогие. Вчера у меня был день рождения* и брат** подарил мне два билета на спектакль на Бродвее. Я пригласил Гришу. Мы встретились <u>за час до</u> спектакля в маленьком итальянском ресторане <u>не далеко от</u> театра. Мы поужинали, и всё было очень вкусно. Мы пришли в театр за десять минут до начала спектакля. Спектакль был отличный. Это была пьеса*** по роману Пристли. Мой любимый актёр играл главную роль. После выступления, публика долго аплодировала. Мне очень понравился спектакль и весь вечер.**** Это был отличный день рождения.

*__Russians say__ Вчера у меня был день рождения. **Russians do not say** "вчера был мой день рождения" **You should not either. Say it right, and sound authentic.**

No need for **мой because it is assumed. Americans overuse the possessive pronouns when they speak Russian. Get used to curbing your possessive pronoun habit.

***The verb here will agree with the "predicate" looking part of the sentence. This sort of sentence might be called "equationary;" the Это is on one side of the equals sign and the verb "to be" and noun on the other. The form of the verb "to be" will agree with the noun in number and gender.

****Here is the question about plural subjects and singular verbs. The subject seems to be plural "спектакль и весь вечер" but the verb is singular. This is not a point to have a heart attack because the expected agreement is missing, just learn to accept it. Basically, the verb takes its number here from the first element.

7.42

1. Саша, который подарил канделябр доктору, был очень доволен.

2. Доктор не знал, что делать с канделябром, который подарил Саша.

3. Отец Саши, который покупал старинную бронзу, продавал её любителям.

4. Канделябр, который купил отец Саши, был из старинной бронзы.

5. У людей, которые покупают произведения искусств, много денег.

6. Мы видели эту скульптуру, которую сделал известный русский скульптор Антакольский, в Третьяковской галерее.

Урок 8:   Письменные задания

stem	чу́вствова+	боле́й+
infinitive	чу́вствовать	боле́ть
non-past		
я	чу́вствую	боле́ю
ты	чу́вствуешь	боле́ешь
он,она́,оно́	чу́вствует	боле́ет
мы	чу́вствуем	боле́ем
вы	чу́вствуете	боле́ете
они́	чу́вствуют	боле́ют
past		
он	чу́вствовал	боле́л
она́	чу́вствовала	боле́ла
они́	чу́вствовали	боле́ли

им	здоровье	болезнь
вин	здоровье	болезнь
род	здоровья	болезни
дат	здоровью	болезни
пред	о здоровье	о болезни
твор	здоровьем	болезнью
им		болезни
вин		болезни
род		болезней
дат		болезням
пред		о болезнях
твор		болезнями

8.4
1. больны, 2. больна, 3.болен, 4. больны, 5.болен (больна), 6.болен, 7.больна

8.6
1. болеет, 2.болеют, 3.заболеешь, 4.заболел, 5.болею, 6.болеет, 7.заболела, болеет

8.8
1. ему плохо. 2. Ей плохо. 3. Им плохо. 4. Нам плохо 5. Тебе плохо? 6. Линде плохо? 7. Джеффу плохо?

8.9

Неделю назад я заболел. У меня болела голова, горло болело и была температура. У меня был кашель. Я чувствовал себя очень плохо. Я ходил к врачу, и он мне сказал, что у меня грипп* и что я должен лежать в постели и принимать лекарство. Сегодня я чувствую себя лучше. Горло у меня больше не болит, голова больше не болит и у меня нормальная температура.

*Notice that there is no past tense here since Russian has different rules for reported speech.

8.12

   This exercise reinforces the use of the averbial **так** in contrast to **такой**.

1. Сегодня так плохо на улице.

—Да, сегодня такая плохая погода.

8.13

б.1. Когда врач осматривал больного он спрашивал, как он себя чувствует.

2. Сначала врач осмотрел больного и потом выписал лекарство.

3. Сначала молодой человек выпил лекарство и потом лёг спать.

4. Пока мы пили чай, мы разговаривали.

5. Сначала мы выпили чай и потом пошли гулять.

6. Сначала он вошел в комнату, потом он снял пальто и потом повесил его в шкаф.

7. В то время как они вешали тёплые вещи в шкаф, они говорили о погоде.

8.18

1. Я хочу есть, потому что я сегодня не успел пообедать.

   Я сегодня не успел пообедать, поэтому я хочу есть.

2. Линда заболела, потому что она сняла теплое пальто.

   Линда сняла теплое пальто, поэтому она заболела.

8.19

1. Если завтра будет холодно, (то) мы не пойдем в бассейн.

2. Если в воскресенье будет дождь, (то) мы не поедем на дачу.

3. Если вы придете ко мне, (то) я покажу вам новые фотографии.

4. Если завтра будет хорошая погода, (то) мы поедем в зоопарк.

8.23

1. Если завтра будет хорошая погода, мы пойдём в парк.

2. Он приехал в Вашингтон недавно, поэтому он плохо знает город.

3. Мы сидели дома весь вечер, потому что шел дождь.

4. Если у меня будет свободное время, я пойду на концерт.

5. Если я буду хорошо себя чувствовать, я приду к тебе вечером.

8.24

1. Если бы вы мне дали свой телефон, я бы вам позвонила.

2. Если бы мы достали билеты, мы пошли бы на премьеру.

3. Если бы он купил мне билет, я бы поехала на выставку.

4. Если бы они пригласили Анну, она бы пришла.

5. Если бы врач выписал рецепт, Ира купила бы лекарство.

1. Мы бы гуляли весь вечер в парке, если бы не пошел сильный дождь.
2. Мы бы съездили на море, если бы не было холодно.
3. Я бы тебе позвонил, если бы не пришел поздно.
4. Оля бы пошла с нами, если бы она не заболела.
5. Антон ответил бы на твое письмо, если бы он не потерял адрес.

8.27

1. Она бы пела, если бы у нее не болело горло.
2. Мы бы ходили в библиотеку, если бы она не была закрыта.
3. Он бы покупал дорогое вино, если бы у него были деньги.
4. Я ходил бы по магазинам, если бы у меня было свободное время.
5. Он бы приходил к нам, если бы он на нас не обиделся.

8.31

1. Врач сказал, чтобы я принимал лекарство три раза в день.
2. Врач сказал, чтобы я полежал дня три.
3. Олег сказал мне, чтобы я не ходил без шапки.
4. Линда попросила Наташу, чтобы она сходила в аптеку и купила лекарство.
5. Миша сказал Свете, чтобы она посмотрела по телевизору прогноз погоды на завтра.

8.33а

-Что с тобой, ты плохо выглядишь.
-Не знаю, я не хорошо чувствую себя.
-Что у тебя болит?
-У меня голова болит, и мне очень холодно.
-Может быть у тебя температура?
-Может быть, не знаю.
-Тебе надо сходить к врачу.

б

-Мне сказали, что ты ездил в Петербург.
-Да, я был в Петербурге на прошлой неделе.
-Тебе понравилось.
-Да, очень. Петербург очень красивый город.
-А какая была там погода?
-Сначала было прохладно, а потом стало тепло.
-А дождя не было?
-Нет, не было.
-Вам повезло. В Петербурге часто идёт дождь. (Часто бывает дождь)

8.34

Я болею уже неделю, и мне очень скучно. Врач сказал, что у меня бронхит, и сказал, чтобы я лежал (в постели) две недели. Я читаю много, смотрю телевизор, и разговариваю по телефону с друзьями. Боб заходил позавчера и принёс мне очень вкусный торт и бултыку французского вина. Вино я не могу пить*, потому, что принимаю антибиотики. Боб мне рассказывал обо всех уроках. Была лекция русского профессора в среду об экологическом кризисе в России. Профессор Петров, который преподаёт в нашем университете в этом семестре**, очень интересный человек. Я хочу познакомиться с ним, когда буду чувствовать себя лучше.*** Еслу завтра буду чувствовать себя лучше, пойду на урок. Боб сказал, что если я не буду лежать ещё несколько дней, я не выздоровлю. (что я должен лежать ещё несколько дней, а то не выздоровлю.)***

*Word order here is important. Since the wine has been mentioned already it is considered "old information" and is place at the beginning of the utterance. New information is placed later. In this way the Russian speaker knows that the sentence is speaking of "the wine" as opposed to "wine in general."

    A semester is longer than a day, so "in a semester" is expressed with **в+ the prepositional.

    ***This sentence is tough. Try and render it in Russian so that the gist is conveyed. Use constructions you know..

8.35
1. ... которую вылечил....
2. ...которые желают ...
3. ...которая не любит...
4. ... которые болеют гриппом...
5. ... которое выписал врач.
6. ... который лежал в постели.

Урок 9:   Письменные задания

9.4

Read the instructions carefully. This is a tricky point for English speakers because, for some strange reason, we don't use a prepositonal construction after the verb "to play"; we have a direct object. The Russians have a prepositonal construction—remember that. What's worse for us is that they have two different prepositional constructions, depending on if they want to say that that they are playing a game or an instrument. Since we want to speak Russian like the Russians do and not like Americans we must remember that to play an instrument is **играть** plus **на** plus the prepositional case "I play the guitar" **Я играю на гитаре**. To play a game is **играть** plus **в** plus the accusative case "I play basketball" is **Я играю в баскетбол**. It grates on teachers' nerves to no end when students forget the prepositional so don't forget it, please. For a number of sports activities Russians use the single verb construction **кататься** plus **на** plus the prepositional. The English equivalents for these constructions are varied. Sometimes we say "to go skiing" or "to ski" or "to go biking" or "to bike" or "to go skating" or "to skate" or "to go riding". Here the nouns **лыжи, коньки, велосипед** use this construction. Skiis and skates are plural so make sure you say **кататься на лыжах, кататься на коньках**. Otherwise the exercise should present few problems.

9.5b

This exercises has you review the forms of the instrumental. Here the instrumental of the objects offered is: бегом, рыбной ловлей, современной литературой, футболом, музыкой, плаванием, хоккеем, фотографией, марками.

9.6.a
1. Он любит плавать.   2. Она любит танцевать   3. Они любят петь 4. Она любит фотографировать.   5. Они любят рисовать.
б.
1. Он часто пла́вает.   2. Она часто танцу́ет.   3. Они часто пою́т.
        4. Она часто фотографи́рует.   5. Они часто рису́ют.

9.8
Она сама хорошо танцу́ет.
Они сами хорошо пою́т
Он сам хорошо рису́ет
Она сама хорошо пла́вает.

9.9

Some practice with the phrase "To spend time" in the third person, the prepositional and what one likes to do.

9.10

These all practice the unprefixed verbs of motion. ходить/идти, ездить/ехать should be familiar to you. For the conjugations of all of these verbs please refer to page 386 of your text.

   1. плавать   2. плаваете 3. плавать   4. плывут, плывёт, плывёт.

   2. ходить [Yes, I know, didn't we just say that you use кататься? Here we see we can also use ходить if the skiing is cross country, at least.], ходил, ходить

   2. идёте, идём, идёте, иду
   3.1. бегает, 2. бегать   3. бежит   бежит

4.1 ездил, ездил[I know, I know, didn't we just say that you use кататься with things like bikes and skiis.. Here we see we can also use ездить. Don't panic; enjoy it.]   2. едет, едет.

9.11

1. Марию интересует история искусств.   2. Сергея интерестует театр. 3. Их интересует современная поэзия. 4. Сашу интересует техника. 5. Его сына интересует компьютер 6. Её интерецуются народные танцы. 7. Его интересуют машины.

9.12

1. Меня интересует рок-музыка. 4. Её интересует классический балет

9.13

Я снова начала плавать на этой неделе. Я уже несколько лет занимаюсь плаванием и плаваю почти каждый день. Но в прошлом месяце я была больна (был болен) и не плавал(а). Обычно я хожу в басейн с моей подругой Анна. Анна очень хорошо плавает. Она занимается плаванием с детства. В нашем университете много различных секций и клубов. Есть секции аэробики, гимнастики, каратэ, тениса. Многие студенты играют в футбол и в баскетбол. Наша университетская команда по футболу (Футбольная команда нашего университета) очень хорошая.

Мой друг (моя подруга) увлекается фотографией. Он много фотографирует. У него несколько очень красивых снимок (фотографий). Недавно мы были на интересной выставке профессиональных фотографов. После выставки, я ему сказал(а), что ему надо (он должен) организовать выставку своих работ. Но он ответил, что он просто любитель.

9.14

stem	привыкай+	привык[ну]+	отвыкай+	отвык[ну]+
infinitive	привыка́ть	привы́кнуть	отвыка́ть	отвы́кнуть
non-past				
я	привыка́ю	привы́кну	отвыка́ю	отвы́кну
ты	привыка́ешь	привы́кнешь	отвыка́ешь	отвы́кнешь
он,она́,оно́	привыка́ет	привы́кнет	отвыка́ет	отвы́кнет
мы	привыка́ем	привы́кнем	отвыка́ем	отвы́кнем
вы	привыка́ете	привы́кнете	отвыка́ете	отвы́кнете
они́	привыка́ют	привы́кнут	отвыка́ют	отвы́кнут
past				
он	привыка́л	привык	отвыка́л	отвык
она́	привыка́ла	привыкла	отвыка́ла	отвыкла
они́	привыка́ли	привыкли	отвыка́ли	отвыкли
imperative	привыка́й	привы́кни	отвыка́й	отвы́кни

9.15

1.Откуда ты идёшь

Я иду из парка

Ты бегал?

Да, я привык(ла) бегать каждый день

121

9.16

1.Олег устал потому что он давно не плавал и отвык плавать.

2.Катя устала потому что она давно не занимается аэробикой и отвыкла занимается аэробикой.

3.Том устал потому что он давно не ходил пешком и отвык ходить пешком.

9.18

1. —Почему Ира не поёт? —Ей надоело петь.
2. Почему Нина не танцует? —Ей надоело танцевать.
3. Почему вы не играете? —Мне (Нам) надоело играть.
4. Почему он не слушает? —Ему надоело слушать.
5. Почему Алэн не работает? Ему надоело работать

9.19

1. Это одна из моих знакомых.
2. Я встретила одного из своих знакомых.
3. Мы увидели одного из наших преподавателей.
4. Я звонил одному из моих друзей.
5. Я написала письмо одной из своих подруг.
6. Я вспомнил об одном из своих друзей.
7. Мы ходили на матч с одной из наших знакомых.
8. ... с одним из моих друзей.

9.20

В детстве я собирал(а) камни. Я их искал везде. Я собрал(а) огромную коллекцию, и у меня было много красивых камней. Но мне надоело собрать камни и я увлёкся (увлеклась) спортом и забыл о коллекции. Недавно один из моих знакомых (приятелей, друзей) увидел мою коллекцию и сказал, что он стоит много.

9.21

1. на кларнете 2. в футбол 3. в теннис 4. на рояле. 5. в хоккей 6. на скрипке. 7. в карты.

9.22

1. по боксу 2. по волейболу 3. по гимнастике 4. по шахматам 5. по плаванию 6. по теннису.

9.23

которая в прошлом месяце ездила в Бостон.

в которой ... раньше играл одиз из моих знакомых.

в которой ... мой брат был тренером

с которой ... недавно играла наша команда

о которой ... писали в университетской газете.

9.24

Играли . играли, проиграли, выиграл, играет, сыграла, проиграла.

9.25

В нашей семье все увлекаются музыкой. Мой дедушка был профессиональным музыкантом. Он играл на фортепиано. Мой отец музыкант-любитель. Он работает в банке, но всё своё свободное время он проводит в джасс клубе. Он играет на саксафоне. Мой брат очень хорошо играет на флейте. Моя сестра играет на пианино. И я раньше играл на пианино, но оно мне надоело и я бросил играть. Теперь я играю только на гитаре. У матери очень красивый голос, и она очень хорошо поёт.

9.28

1. Я болею за канадскую команду. 6. Мы болеем за американского теннисиста.

9.29

1. Наша команда выиграла со счётом четыре два. Их команда проиграла со счётом два четыре.

9.31

1. Сергей сказал мне, что сегодня ... Сергей сказал мне, чтобы я посмотрел сегодня ....
2. Она сказал Сергею, что она будет ждать его у входа... Она попросила Сергея, чтобы он подождал её у входа ...
3. Миша сказал нам, что мы можем доехать ...
Миша попросил нас, чтобы мы объяснили ему как доехать до...
4. Маша сказала, что она уже купила ...
Маша попросила меня, чтобы я купил(а)...
5. Сын сказал отцу, что он не умеет играть ...
Сын попросил отца, чтобы он показал ему, как играть в шахматы.

9.32

1. что, чтобы. 2. что, чтобы 3. чтобы, что. 4. что, чтобы.

9.34

Деньги, денег, деньгами, деньгах, деньги, деньгам

9.35

детях, детьми, детей, дети, детям, детях

9.38

1. Дети, которые сидят за столом, за которым обедают, играли в лотто.
2. Соня, девочка лет шести, которая играет ради процесса игры, хохочет и хлопает в ладоши.
3. которые играют
4. которые бегают
5. которые потеряли
6. которая выиграла партию

9.39

—Привет, как дела?

—Привет, так себе. Я не очень хорошо чувствую себя.

—Что-нибудь болит?

—Нет, ничего не болит, я просто очень устал.

—А ты занимаешься спортом?

—Нет, у меня нет свободного времени.

—Жаль, я начал плавать недавно, и теперь я чувствую себя гораздо лучше.

—Я не умею плавать

—Тогда ты должен бегать или кататься на велосипеде.

—Привет

—Здравствуй. Куда ты идешь?

—Я иду в бассейн.

—В бассейн. Ты не любишь плавать!

—Правда, я не люблю. Но сегодня соревнование по плаванию и мой друг участвует.

—Так что ты будешь болеть за него?

—Конечно.

—Что это за музыка?

—Это играет мой сосед. Он играет на гитаре очень хорошо.

—Он музыкант?

—Нет, он не профессиональный музыкант, он любитель. Ты играешь на гитаре?

—Нет, я ни на чём не играю, но я очень люблю слушать музыку.

—Хочешь, я тебя с ним познакомлю?

—Да, я бы хотел познакомиться с ним.

Урок 10: Письменные задания

10.1c

1. путешествовать
2. путеводитель
3. спутники
4. путешественник
5. путь

d.. 1. видный
2. видно
3. свидетель
4. видел
5. вид
6. видит
7. видимо
8. видно
9. видны

10.4

Мы гуляли по лесу.
Мы с родителями путешествовали по Европе.
Мои друзья ездили по Крыму.
Наша группа ходила по горам.

10.9

Этим летом мы с родителями ездили на каникули. Мы ездили на море. Мы были на Гавайских островах. Я очень доволен поездкой. Всё было замечательно. Мы жили в хорошей гостинице на берегу моря. Мне особенно понравилось море. Я никогда в жизни не видел такого синего моря. Там было так хорошо, что мы никуда не ходили, и я всё время лежал на пляже. Я много плавал.

10.16. а

1. Джон давно хотел поехать в Суздаль, и наконец, в прошлом месяце съездил туда.
2. Карен давно хотела поехать в Киев, и наконец, в июне съездила туда.
3. Борис давно хотел поехать в Нью Йорк, и наконец летом съездил туда.
4. Ира давно хотела поехать в Аризону, и наконец весной съездила туда.
5. Мы давно хотели поехать в Японию, и наконец зимой съездили туда.
6. Я давно хотел поехать на Гавайские острова, и наконец, в сентябре съездил туда.

б.

1. Бетси давно хотела пойти в Третьяковскую галерею, и наконец в среду, она сходила туда.
2. Кира давно хотела пойти в музей Пушкина, и наконец позавчера, она сходила туда.
3. Олег давно хотел пойти в музей Гуггенхайма, и наконец в субботу сходил туда.
4. Мы давно хотели пойти в Метрополитен, и наконец, в воскресенье, мы сходили туда.
5. Я давно хотел(а) пойти в Эрмитаж, и наконец во вторник, сходил(а) туда.

10.18

На прошлой неделе приезжали ко мне друзья из Петербурга. Мы решили поехать в Аризону, в Большой Каньон. Мы полетели в Финекс. Там мы взяли на прокат машину и поехали в Большой Каньон. Я сам никогда не был на Большом Каньоне. Я никогда в жизни не видел такой красоты. Друзьям очень понравилась поездка.

10.20

1. Они походили попарку и пошли в музей.
2. Степан походил по центру города и пошёл в магазин
3. Оля походила по берегу моря и пошла в аквариум.
4. Я походил по монастырю и пошёл в гостиницу.
5. Мы походили по зоопарку и пошли в кино.

10.21

1. Я походил по парку и пошёл на море.
2. Мы поездили по центру города и поехали в театр.
3. Я поездил по магазинам и поехал в гостиницу.
4. Мы походили по музею и пошли в кафе.
5. Я походил по выставке и пошёл в бассейн.

10.23

Я хотел походить немного по зоопарку, но мне там так понравилось, что я проходил там полдня.
2. Они хотели походить немного по выставке, но им там так понравилось, что я проходили там всё утро.
3. Джефф хотел походить немного по монастырю, но ему там так понравилось, что я проходил там весь вечер.
4. Кристи хотела походить немного по зоопарку, но ей там так понравилось, что я проходила там два часа.
5. Мы хотели походить немного по парку, но нам там так понравилось, что мы проходил там полдня.

10.24

1. походили
2. проходили
3. поездили
4. проездили
5. походили
6. проходили

10.25

1.Что вы привезли с Урала?
Я привёз (привезла́) красивый аметист.
2. Что вы привезли из Италии?
 Я привёз (привезла́) золотой кольцо
3. Что вы привезли из Африки
Я привёз (привезла́) деревянную статуэтку.
4.Что вы привезли с Байкал?
Я привёз (привезла́) богатую коллекцию камней.
5 Что вы привезли из Америки?
Я привёз (привезла́) замечательную фотографию.

10.26

1. Мой друг привёз мне попугая из Африки.

2 Мать привезла нам плакаты из Парижа

3 Моя подруга привезла своей сестре Италии

4 Иван привёз Ире аметист с Урала

5 Мы привезли родителям картину из Индии.

6 Они привезли нам книги из Москвы.

7 Я привёз (привезла́) вам пластиники из Петербург.

10.27

ви́дно всё озеро

видна́ вся старая часть

видны́ все соборы Кремля

видна́ вся набережная

ви́ден весь Петербург

видны́ все горы

ви́ден весь остров.

10.28

Вчера я вернулся (вернулась) из Италии. Мы были там всего только три недели. Мы полетели в Рим в субботу. В первый день мы поездили по Риму немного утром а потом поехали в Флоренцию на автобусе. Мне очень понравилась Флоренция. Мы проходили весь день по городу. Мы вернулись в гостиницу позно вечером. В среду мы поехали в Венецию. Самое замечательное в Венеции—это каналы. Я привёз (привезла́) много фотографий с поездки. Я очень доволен (довольна) поездкой.

10.29

После того, как (Когда) мы поднялись на г... После того, как (Когда) мы пообедали,...

После того, как (Когда) ребята погуляли в лесу,...

После того, как(Когда) Джон позвонил на вокзал, .

 После того, как(Когда) она купила,...

б. Когда он уезжал отдыхать,...

Когда дети купались в озере,...

Когда я возвращалась домой, ...

Когда она читала его письмо, ...

Когда мы сидели на берегу моря,...

10.30

Ира спросила Алана, понравилось ли ему на Урале.

Бренда спросила Сашу, любит ли он (она) Петербург.

Наташа спросила Джона, доволен ли он своей поездкой на Байкал.

Ира спросила Алана, привёз ли он сувениры из Ильменского заповедника.

Саша спросил Бренду, гуляла ли она ночью по Петербургу.